HAPPY CUSTOMERS EVERYWHERE

ALSO BY BERND SCHMITT

Experiential Marketing

Customer Experience Management

Big Think Strategy

HAPPY CUSTOMERS EVERYWHERE

HOW YOUR BUSINESS CAN PROFIT FROM THE INSIGHTS OF POSITIVE PSYCHOLOGY

BERND SCHMITT

WITH GLENN VAN ZUTPHEN

palgrave
macmillan

First published in 2012 by PALGRAVE MACMILLAN® in the United
States—a division of St. Martin's Press LLC, 175 Fifth Avenue, New York,
NY 10010.

Where this book is distributed in the UK, Europe and the rest of the
world, this is by Palgrave Macmillan, a division of Macmillan Publishers
Limited, registered in England, company number 785998, of Houndmills,
Basingstoke, Hampshire RG21 6XS.

Palgrave Macmillan is the global academic imprint of the above companies
and has companies and representatives throughout the world.

Palgrave® and Macmillan® are registered trademarks in the United States,
the United Kingdom, Europe and other countries.

ISBN: 978-230-11645-0

Library of Congress Cataloging-in-Publication Data
Schmitt, Bernd.
    Happy customers everywhere : how your business can profit from the
insights of positive psychology / Bernd Schmitt with Glenn Van Zutphen.
        p.   cm.
    Includes index.
    ISBN 978-0-230-11645-0
    1. Consumer behavior. 2. Consumption (Economics)—Psychological
aspects. 3. Consumers' preferences. I. Van Zutphen, Glenn. II. Title.
HF5415.32.S355   2012
658.8'342—dc23

                                                            2011042923

A catalogue record of the book is available from the British Library.

Design by Letra Libre Inc.

First edition: April 2012

10 9 8 7 6 5 4 3 2 1

Printed in the United States of America.

CONTENTS

PREFACE

Customer happiness is a new and exciting business concept. It is closely related to the established concepts of customer satisfaction, customer delight and the Net Promoter Score, yet it goes far beyond them in significance.

In particular, customer happiness focuses on the positive emotional aspects of purchase and consumption. I am presenting here, for the first time to a business audience, the key insights of the new field of positive psychology and how they can help managers and marketers develop methods for making customers happy.

Customer happiness is also central to customer experience and creativity—topics that I have written about in my previous books, including *Experiential Marketing, Customer Experience Management* and *Big Think Strategy*. As I will show, customer happiness results from joyful, meaningful and engaging experiences, and customer happiness campaigns are most successful when they are executed in creative and innovative ways.

I have tried to strike an engaging tone by mixing concepts and methods with practical examples of customer happiness campaigns from around the world.

We will begin and end in Singapore. Along the way, you will encounter case examples from both the US (W Hotels, Whole Foods Market and Coca-Cola) and everywhere else. You will read about a call center in Brazil, a children's theme park in Colombia and a movie theater company in Mexico. I will feature examples from Europe (BMW in Germany, Le Pain Quotidien in Belgium and Virgin in the UK, for example) and from Asia (Samsung and Yuhan-Kimberly in South Korea; Uniqlo in Japan; Procter &Gamble's efforts in India and China).

There will be many examples from B2C (business-to-consumer) companies, and some from B2B (business-to-business) companies. Throughout the book, I will discuss new and social media. I will feature cases from a wide range of product categories, from the Prius car to Brita water filters, from fast moving consumer goods (FMCG) to medical technology equipment. We will talk about yoga and lingerie, about chocolates and couple massagers (aka vibrators). In the last two chapters, I will explore how companies can help their employees become happy at work (and, in turn, make customers happy), and what governments can do to make their citizens happy.

I hope that you will enjoy the reading experience and that the concepts and methodologies of the book will be useful to your business.

ACKNOWLEDGMENTS

Many people have helped and supported me in writing this book. First of all, Glenn van Zutphen, who wrote the book with me, has spent numerous hours on this project. While the idea for the book and key concepts may all be mine, Glenn contributed a casual and cool writing style and also researched and wrote up several case studies. Working with him was an enjoyable and fully collaborative process.

Shireen Seow has discussed with me the concepts of the book and read the manuscript several times. Shireen is a thorough and creative thinker, reader and writer. I have greatly benefitted from her comments and support, and I thank her very much for that.

Matt Quint, who works with me at the Center on Global Brand Leadership at Columbia Business School, has done some of the interviews for the book and provided background research support together with Justin Epstein. My assistant at the Institute on Asian Consumer Insight in Singapore, Rachel Samuil, helped with the final editing of the manuscript. Finally, I thank Emily Carleton, senior editor at Palgrave Macmillan, and her boss, Airié Stuart, for believing in this book and supporting me.

Did I miss anybody? Yes, I did. I must also acknowledge the help of an eleven-year-old boy, Thomas Fujii Schmitt, who has read several chapters. I feel that if a young man like him does not get the core message and enjoy the book, then the author is to blame.

1

THE CASE FOR
CUSTOMER HAPPINESS

'm sitting in a café at the corner of Orchard and Scotts roads in Singapore after a long flight from New York. The iced latte is just what I need to slake the weary, jet-lagged feeling that's defining this moment. Surrounding me are sparkling shopping malls, massive five-storey-tall outdoor TV screens, restaurants, hotels and movie theaters. Luxury brand names spill out of boutiques onto the sidewalk as easily as the shoppers who flit from store to store in search of retail satisfaction.

Singapore is one of the epicenters of shopping, not just in Asia, but globally. Of course, nearby Hong Kong deserves a nod for its stretch of malls from Pacific Place to Central and into the International Finance Centre of Hong Kong Island, and for its massive retail malls in Tsim Sha Tsui. Expansive shopping malls have also been developed in Beijing and Shanghai. The Ginza shopping district in Tokyo has been revamped. The United Arab

Emirates' shopping malls are following suit. In South America, too, I have seen glitzy new malls. In terms of sheer, over-the-top, slick consumerism, Singapore is at least equal to—or surpasses— all of them, including the Mall of America in Minnesota, Fifth Avenue in New York City, the Golden Mile in Chicago and any European shopping street.

There are many nationalities sitting around me. I listen to excited shoppers talking in different languages about what they've just purchased. Everyone seems to be making the most of their lattes, cappuccinos and warmed muffins before beginning the next round of retail therapy. People seem to enjoy that sort of experience: relaxing between shopping. More than that, and this may seem strange, they look—and sound—happy. There seem to be happy customers everywhere!

How can this be? Haven't philosophers over the centuries and numerous writers and psychologists argued and proved that materialism is bad for us? That shopping distracts us from achieving our true goals in life? That it's superficial and that commercial consumption can't create happiness?

Maybe these authors were missing something. Maybe people can experience happiness as consumers. Maybe it is possible, as the ads of stores surrounding me proclaim, to "find happiness in shoes," to "find happiness *within*" (ice cream, that is) and to "forget love" entirely and "fall in chocolate." After all, how do you explain consumers' obsession with Apple products? How do you explain why people may go out of their way to find something as mundane as the right hair conditioner? And doesn't an argument over Coca-Cola versus Pepsi sound like a lovers' quarrel?

Consider McDonald's "Happy Meal."[1] Launched more than 30 years ago in June 1979, the "Happy Meal" is viewed by some as a gimmick to get young consumers hooked on the company's burgers and fries with a cheap toy. Nonetheless, in its approach McDonald's was far ahead of its time in considering the notion of customer happiness.

The usual explanation, brand preference, just doesn't seem to do full justice to what's going on. Some consumers do not just *prefer* a brand; they seem truly happy about their purchases and are genuinely in love with the brand.

The core premise of this book is that shopping for goods, buying them and consuming them can indeed make people happy. While consumerism and marketing are often critiqued as distracting individuals from the pursuit of finding happiness in their lives, if done right and with a genuine interest in consumers as real human beings, commercial activities and marketing can enhance an individual's well-being, quality of life and life satisfaction.

Specifically, shopping, buying and consuming *can* result in pleasurable moments and sometimes in meaningful and engaging experiences that create happiness. Moreover, customer happiness does not need to be a passing mood. It can last and create an intimate and ongoing close relationship between a company and its customers. This relationship can strengthen the brand and result in future revenue.

My argument is entirely consistent with conceptual developments and empirical research over the last decade in the field of psychology. Thus, throughout the book, I will use psychological concepts to develop strategies and methods that can lead to customer happiness.

HAPPINESS: THE NEW APPROACH
TO CUSTOMER BEHAVIOR

Nowadays, customer behavior is being approached on a different level and more deliberately than ever. Companies seek to build close relationships with their customers and not merely market to them using transparent advertising messages. They want customers to experience pleasure, find meaning in their products and services and be fully engaged online. Companies want to connect with their customers on an emotional level: they want them to fall in love with their products and services. They want to appear on customers' blogs and tweets and on their social networking sites.

As a result, companies today are spending big money—as well as much effort and time—to develop happiness campaigns and to incorporate them into their customer-oriented business strategies.

In 2012, following the success of its McCafé, McDonald's will accelerate a USD 2.4 billion program to rebuild, relaunch, and refurbish thousands of its restaurants around the world.[2] In what it's calling the first restaurant makeover since the mid-1970s, the company's "Experience Engineer" and VP of Concept and Design, Dennis Weil, has devised four concepts for seating zones: chilling out, working, casual dining and group events. The cool revamp, with its clean lines and modern design, is an effort to make McDonald's restaurants a place where people will come to hang out. It's supposed to be a sort of fast-food town square, a place where people will nurture relationships that researchers tell us are central to happiness. The plan appears to be a winner: sales are up 6 to 7 percent at locations that already sport the new look. The company is banking on the fact that the new McDonald's will change behavior and draw in people for a mutually shared happy experience, rather than the traditional pattern of pick-up-and-go.

CUSTOMER HAPPINESS IS EVERYWHERE

Customer happiness is no longer just associated with what you eat or drink. Hotels, car manufacturers and life insurance companies are trying to make us happy. Consumer electronics manufacturers are jumping on the bandwagon. Happiness is also no longer limited to large firms. Ask any Pilates studio or private yoga instructor: they all want to make you happy, too.

The concept may be coming to your local bank as well if you live in Australia. In 2007, the Bank of Western Australia in Perth, commonly known as Bankwest, challenged its larger competitors in the Australian banking industry to explain why banking can't be more positive. This led to its "Happy Banking" and "Banking Refreshed" advertising campaigns.[3] The ads showed various happiness experts helping the bank to understand what would make customers happy and how to improve service.

The retail campaign entailed the creation of 160 new branches across four states. According to Bankwest, from 2007 to 2010 the "Happy Banking" campaign helped double the number of customers, from 450,000 to over one million.

If today's marketers want to empathize and connect with customers, it's hard to imagine getting any closer to the target consumer than Procter & Gamble's (P&G) campaign for the Always brand of feminine hygiene products, "Have a Happy Period." As its dedicated website says: "This is the time of the month that's all about you. So be your own best friend. Make it your mantra to indulge yourself and celebrate 'beinggirl.'"[4]

The website hyperlinks to another website, seemingly aimed at pubescent girls and their concerns about menstruation, relationships and other pangs of adolescence.[5] Inspired by the recent wellness trend, the "Have a Happy Period" page gives tips on how to, well, have the best period ever. The website offers the following practical suggestions:

- Make a hot cup of herbal tea.
- Melt away stress by taking a warm bath with candlelight and bath oil.
- Take a walk or a yoga class.
- Watch TV with a heating pad on your stomach.
- Consider dry heating pads—warm wraps that will let you leave the house and participate fully in your life.
- Sleep in late on the weekends and serve yourself breakfast in bed.
- Satisfy your cravings for a particular food.

It's important to note that this campaign, which started in 2007, got a lot of flak from journalists and letters from some indignant women, including this open missive to P&G from a blogger in Austin, Texas:

> "Sir, please inform your accounting department that, effective immediately, there will be an $8 drop in monthly profits, for I have chosen to take my maxi-pad business elsewhere. And though I will certainly miss your Flexi-Wings, I will not for one minute miss your brand of condescending bullshit. And that's a promise I will keep. Always."[6]

Yet, despite these and other subpar reviews of the campaign, it seems to be quite successful. Infegy's Social Radar social media monitoring and analytics system says the "Happy Period" campaign has remained overwhelmingly positive since it first appeared in March 2007. The campaign probably would not have worked 10 or 12 years ago, when customers did not desire such a personal relationship with manufacturers and brands, especially involving such a sensitive topic. Its success today shows how important the concept of happiness has become in people's lives.

Even national governments are getting in on the act. My colleague at Columbia Business School, Professor Joseph Stiglitz, a Nobel Prize–winning economist and former World Bank chief economist, is pushing governments to make sure they consider the happiness of citizens as equal to, if not more important than, the mere measure of gross domestic product (GDP).[7] He believes that looking at GDP without considering the cost of economic progress (environmental degradation, for example) gives a false picture, and he urges governments to look at both the assets and liabilities on society's balance sheet.

The idea behind this new approach is that after a certain point, rising national wealth stops making its citizens any happier. This effect, called the Easterlin Paradox, has raised the question "What does it take, then, to make people happy?" In response, "Happiness Economics" has emerged as a discipline over the past 15 years.[8] Combining economics with psychology and sociology, it quantitatively studies topics like well-being, quality of life and life satisfaction in addition to the traditional notions of wealth, such as income or gross domestic product.

In late 2010, the government of the UK announced that it would start measuring people's psychological and environmental well-being, making it one of the first countries to monitor the happiness of its citizens. The governments of France and Canada are considering similar measures. Let's see whether the government of the country that wrote the pursuit of happiness into its Declaration of Independence will start a happiness campaign soon.

HOW IMPORTANT IS HAPPINESS IN B2C AND B2B?

Just like other recent business trends (branding in the 1990s, customer experience in the early 2000s and new media in recent years), customer happiness as a topic first appeared on the agenda of B2C companies. Customer happiness is very important in B2C businesses and is used increasingly for competitive advantage. However, I expect it to be picked up by B2B companies as well since the message is no less useful there.

B2B dealings may involve different products and services and use different criteria for decision making (order time, proximity to a factory, global sourcing system, etc.). But if you are running a B2B business, you should also be concerned with whether your company customers, suppliers and trade customers are happy with your services. After all, the decision maker will be an individual or a group of individuals. Small pleasurable moments during a sales meeting or an immersive experience at a trade show can make a big difference. Also, doing business with a company that shares similar values can be rewarding. Most importantly, you should engage both business customers and end consumers alike to ensure a healthy bottom line.

Many of the benchmark cases and best practices featured in this book will come from B2C. Yet this book also includes B2B examples—like the case of Brainlab, a company that sells medical technology equipment; the Central Asia Group, which explores the use of mobile banking technology in Afghanistan; and IBM's Smaller Planet campaign.

THE PHILOSOPHY AND SCIENCE OF HAPPINESS

Wikipedia defines happiness as "a mental state of well-being characterized by positive emotions ranging from contentment to intense joy." According to psychologist Ed Diener, individuals experience happiness "when they feel many pleasant and few unpleasant emotions, when they are engaged in interesting activities, when they experience many pleasures and few pains, and when they are satisfied with their lives."[9] Because the emotional experience of happiness is often evoked by an event or a person, it may be measured by asking to what degree the event or person (or brand) contributes to happiness, or, reversely, how much an individual might miss the event, person or brand if it were no longer present. Moreover, happiness is a subjective psychological state: what makes people happy differs from person to person. Happiness is often momentary and transient, although it can also persist to the point of becoming a characteristic trait. When we characterize someone as a happy person, we refer to their consistent display of positive emotions and life satisfaction over time.

For two and a half millennia, thinkers like Confucius and Buddha, Socrates and Aristotle and Immanuel Kant and Karl Marx have been philosophizing about what constitutes happiness and/or a "good life." Naturally, their views varied widely. Some advised a "religious life," while others advised us to stay away from religion (Karl Marx wrote that "the first requisite for the happiness of the people is the abolition of religion"). Buddha taught that happiness entails wisdom, and Aristotle proclaimed that happiness is intricately linked to ethical conduct and virtues. We will sort out these different views and examine their relevance to business in chapter 2.

It is also useful to look at modern-day scientific thinking on the topic. The positive psychology movement, in a sense the basis for this book, has put the spotlight on happiness since the beginning of this century. Martin Seligman and Mihaly Csikszentmihalyi, two of its key proponents, consider it as a science of positive subjective experience. The field of positive psychology thus provides an alternative perspective to traditional psychology's decades-long obsession with damage repair and healing. Positive psychology stresses positive experiences (including well-being, contentment, satisfaction, hope, optimism, flow and love), positive individual traits (such as aesthetic sensibility, perseverance, originality and future purpose), and positive institutional values (such as responsibility, civility, tolerance and work ethic). This book will use key concepts of positive psychology to develop business frameworks and tools for creating happy customers.

Why, you might ask, should companies dedicate their limited resources to making customers happy? Aren't they in the business of making money, not spending it on something as elusive as customer happiness? Making customers happy may be an admirable goal. But are we, as business people, now supposed to become therapists, social workers or, to use a more contemporary term, "life coaches" for customers?

Assuming we are even able to devise tools for creating happy customers, how will doing so impact on the bottom line for business?

Make no mistake, there is a business objective here—a big one. Companies don't create happiness campaigns just to be nice. Happy customers provide immense value to a company. Companies want to profit from customer happiness. In other words, companies see dollar signs on customers' happy faces.

The empirical evidence on customer satisfaction, customer delight and the Net Promoter Score, a measure of customer loyalty, indicates that happy customers are of tremendous value to an organization.[10] They become lifetime (or at least longtime) customers and enthusiastically recommend products and services to family, friends and coworkers.

Happy customers can elevate brands to iconic status. Happy customers will even help a firm design new products and volunteer time and effort in promoting the company through their personal websites, blogs and other social media.

Why are happy customers such a gold mine? In the following pages, I will present a model that explains why customer happiness has such positive effects.

THE BUSINESS MODEL OF CUSTOMER HAPPINESS

The model includes two key marketing concepts—customer satisfaction and customer delight.

Customer satisfaction results in a "quiet state of happiness" where the customer feels content. Customer delight is the joy and "wow" factor of happiness. Once customers are happy, they become loyal to a company and are willing to promote its products and services. Thus, the outcome of happiness will be a high Net Promoter Score.

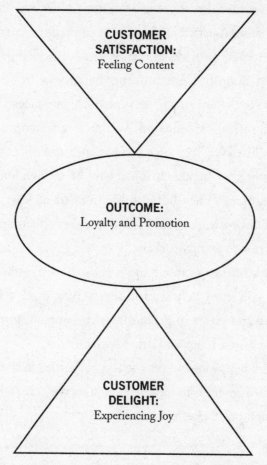

FIGURE 1. THE BUSINESS MODEL OF CUSTOMER HAPPINESS

Let's take a closer look at the components of the model.

CUSTOMER SATISFACTION: FEELING CONTENT

One of the most essential and enduring concepts in marketing is customer satisfaction. When products or services meet or exceed expectations, customers are satisfied. When customer expectations are not met, disappointment and dissatisfaction can lead to complaints or to the customer bad-mouthing the company, product or service.

Expectations play a key role. Clearly, expectations for premium and luxury goods are higher than those for value products. For this reason, even a high-end product, though it may objectively be of better quality than a value product, may sow customer dissatisfaction.

When expectations are met, it creates contentment. When you get what you want with no negative surprises, you relax, you're at peace with the world. There is no need to search for new stimuli. You may even experience gratitude. Thus, customer satisfaction can lead to a quiet sort of happiness.

For example, because of my heavy travel schedule, I value an airline that focuses on time so that I can get in and out of airports and planes quickly. Like most business travelers, I don't want to be stranded in an airport because of a missed connection—even if they try to compensate me by offering lavish personal service and an exquisite layover hotel.

I often fly Lufthansa because it focuses on punctuality, that quintessentially Germanic value. That message is clear throughout the flight: the captain gives frequent updates on departure, weather, arrival and connections. When the flight is delayed, they explain why, tell me how they will try to make up for it and repeat connecting flight information. Lufthansa makes me feel secure and informed; they put me at ease. I feel a sense of contentment knowing that they will try to respect my schedule.

Does Lufthansa induce strong, blissful emotions in me? Am I full of joy when I sit in their seats? Not really. That would take a bit more. Lufthansa simply provides a satisfactory flying experience for me. I expect them to be on time. They do their best to fulfill that expectation and, most of the time, they do.

Many companies use customer satisfaction as a key performance indicator. While sales or market share indicate only how well a firm is performing at the moment, satisfaction is an indicator of how well it may perform in the future because satisfied customers often become a strong base of loyal customers.

Attempting to measure customer satisfaction also sends a simple but important message to customers, namely: "We care about satisfying you."

The usual measure of customer satisfaction is a simple question on a five-point scale. "How satisfied are you? Check '1' for very dissatisfied and '5' for very satisfied, or something in between." For more precision, you can use multiscale measures in which the customer assesses satisfaction with various features of a product or aspects of a service. Consider hotels. How satisfied is a guest with the room, the bed, the linens, the check-in and check-out, the business center, the fitness center, restaurant facilities and so on? These individual aspects of the hotel can then be weighted, and those weighted scores added up into a composite satisfaction score for the hotel.

Most of these satisfaction measures take a common, rational and analytical view of the customer. By nature they are extremely cognitive and left brain–heavy. The assumption of most customer-satisfaction models is that customers think a lot about what they want (from a hotel room, its bed, its linens) and form expectations ahead of time (based on prior product performance or by extending expectations from other brands to a specific brand). They then, presumably, do some sort of mental calculation to determine how satisfied they are.

This sort of measurement omits emotion and surprise. It does not consider customers as full-fledged human beings—with cognitions *and* emotions. It leaves fun out of the equation.

Satisfaction researchers eventually noticed over the years that something was missing. So they added surprise and emotion to the equation, proposing that customers can also experience *delight*—an emotional state that goes far beyond mere customer satisfaction. Delight leads to happiness as well, of course—through joy and novelty rather than through comfort and certainty.

CUSTOMER DELIGHT: EXPERIENCING JOY

In a seminal academic article, three marketing professors, Richard Oliver, Roland Rust and Sajeev Varki, conceptualized customer delight as a high level of satisfaction including pleasure and arousal. They wrote that customer delight results from surprise.[11] It is a strong and positive reaction arising from the unexpected.

As customers, we've all experienced delight and surprise. On a recent shopping trip to IKEA, I was in a rush and forgot to load my purchase of two folding chairs (among many other items I had bought that day) into the car. Ever the absentminded professor, I remembered what I had forgotten the following day. It seemed like a waste of time to ride across town to the store and ask them to search for the inexpensive chairs, so I did nothing. A week later, when I returned to purchase another item, I casually asked about the chairs, expecting nothing. When an employee emerged from the back room holding the two chairs in his hands, I was thrilled! The outcome exceeded my expectation.

Creating a delightful moment doesn't have to be complicated. It can be a personalized message, an unexpected discount or service that comes from the heart. Try to recall a delightful customer encounter of your own. What exactly caused your delight? What part of the experience made you happy?

When companies create a "wow" moment for customers, they engender a very special reaction. They plant a seed in the customer's memory that is easily recalled and that the customer will be motivated to share with family, friends or colleagues, because a joyful experience is a pleasure to share. This is free, personalized advertising for the company that supersedes monetary value. I have shared my IKEA story with many friends and colleagues, both face-to-face and online. I have become an unpaid, third-party cheerleader for IKEA and for other companies that have created a joyful experience for me.

And, of course, the delight you experience leads you back to the company, which will result in your bringing in new customers. This may eventually allow the company to sell its products or services at a premium price.

Some critics suggest that delighting the customer unfairly raises the bar of customer expectations, making it more difficult to satisfy *or* delight them in the long run. This may be so, but customer delight still offers advantages that outweigh this risk. First, these initiatives provide differentiation for the firm in the market. Second, if the company can create customer delight or a customer happiness initiative as a mind-set or strategy (and not as a one-off deal), it will drive innovation that, in turn, keeps customers happy and raises the bar for the competition. Finally, the positive and lasting memories bond the customer to the company.

Isn't this exactly the recipe for Apple's success? Differentiate from the rest of the pack in the consumer electronics industry; always innovate in a consumer-centric way; rely on the bonding provided by the collective memory of the Apple community and the late Steve Jobs.

THE OUTCOME: LOYALTY AND PROMOTION

The Net Promoter Score (NPS) was introduced by Fred Reichheld in a 2003 *Harvard Business Review* article called "The One Number You Need to Grow."[12] It is arguably the most widely used customer metric for loyalty today. A strongly positive NPS indicates that customers are extremely satisfied and delighted— happy, if you will—with the company's product or service and are willing to promote it to others.

The NPS measure asks customers a single question on a 0 to 10 rating scale, "How likely is it that you would recommend our company to a friend or colleague?" Closely note the wording: "recommend" the company (not just telling stories) and "friend or colleague" (not strangers). In your private life or at work, your reputation is at stake, and therefore you recommend very carefully. Most importantly, the NPS is a behavioral rather than perceptual index, asking what customers will *actually* do, rather than what they say they might do.

Based on responses, customers are categorized into one of three groups: Promoters (9–10 rating), Passives (7–8 rating) and Detractors (0–6 rating). The percentage of Detractors is then subtracted from the percentage of Promoters to obtain the NPS. An NPS of +50 is considered to be excellent. The goal is to increase Promoters and decrease Detractors.

Proponents of the approach claim that a company's NPS correlates strongly with revenue growth. The score can also be used to motivate an organization to become more focused on improving products and services.

Businesses rightly love the NPS for its simplicity and benchmarking value. Many academics, on the other hand, are puzzled, because in direct comparison the NPS usually does not outperform other customer satisfaction measures. This comes as no surprise, since voluntary promotion is the behavioral manifestation of a customer's satisfaction and delight. It's the internal glow of happiness driving the behavior. It's the feeling of being understood, of getting what you deserve and of being served with the right products and services. It also goes further: being surprised at times and getting more than expected because this shows the company's extra care and concern for its customers.

Customer satisfaction, customer delight and the NPS are all valuable ideas and metrics. However, from a psychological perspective, they contribute little toward understanding *why* customers are satisfied, delighted or likely to recommend the company. Moreover, from a strategic and tactical business perspective, they provide little advice on how to satisfy customers, how to create surprise and how to turn Detractors into Promoters—that is, how to make customers happy.

Discovering this "why" and "how" is the number-one task of customer insight and customer management executives. Customer management specialists must seek to understand customers' motivations, feelings and behaviors and then develop strategies and tactics that will satisfy customers, delight them and turn them into such enthusiastic supporters that they repeatedly buy and promote the same products and services.

Great businesses have already learned this lesson and apply it often. They have made customer happiness the focus of their entire business.

HAPPINESS AS A BUSINESS FOCUS:
WHOLE FOODS MARKET

In the October 2005 issue of the journal *Reason,* John Mackey, chairman and CEO of Whole Foods Market (WFM), wrote an article called "Rethinking the Social Responsibility of Business."[13] In it he criticized Chicago economist Milton Friedman, who considered profit maximization and shareholder value to be the key goals of a business. "I'm a businessman and a free market libertarian," wrote Mackey, "but I believe that the enlightened corporation should try to create value for *all* of its constituencies."

Mackey is certainly not hostile to profits. At the time he wrote the article, his company had year-on-year sales of more than USD 4.6 billion, net profits of more than USD 160 million, and a market capitalization over USD 8 billion. Compare this to 1980, when he cofounded WFM: The company began with only USD 45,000 and posted USD 250,000 in sales in the first year. Mackey explained:

"We have not achieved our tremendous increase in shareholder value by making shareholder value the primary purpose of our business. In my marriage, my wife's happiness is an end in itself, not merely a means to my own happiness; love leads me to put my wife's happiness first, but in doing so, I also make myself happier. Similarly, the most successful businesses put the customer first, ahead of the investors. In the profit-centered business, customer happiness is merely a means to an end: maximizing profits. In the customer-centered business, customer happiness is an end in itself, and will be pursued with greater interest, passion, and empathy than the profit-centered business is capable of."

Customers are loyal because they believe the company is more than just a supermarket that sells organic produce and natural foods. They appreciate a company that shows concern for the local community and the environment and that offers a good working atmosphere for its "team members" (employees). Anyone who has shopped at WFM knows that it's not inexpensive. But customers have shown their willingness to pay a steep price premium to support the company and its products.

Beyond the mission statement and the exciting stores, how exactly does WFM ensure that customer happiness becomes a self-fulfilling prophecy? Does Mackey's business actually make people happy?

In the 30 years since it began, WFM has built a solid reputation based on the attitude of the founders toward their customers and the fact that they offer products believed to be more healthy than the mainstream supermarket alternatives.

Remember when supermarkets were cavernous places with fluorescent lights bright enough to sting your eyes, cheesy music playing, and a big guy named Irv with meaty arms and a mustache cutting slabs of meat at the back butcher counter? You could go to just about any supermarket in any town in America and know, as you entered the store, where everything would be located. Past the checkout counters, the fresh fruit and produce on the right wall; the meat counter at the back. Turn left and walk all the way across the store (past aisles of dry goods, cereals, snacks, paper goods, greeting cards, pet supplies, laundry detergent and small home fix-it items), and there were the cold cases filled with dairy products, eggs, and eventually frozen veggies, pizzas and ice cream. Make a U-turn back toward the checkout counters, and the wine and beer section was near the front of the store. With minor variations, every grocery store in America had this layout, and this was the way everyone typically bought groceries.

Then WFM turned the status quo on its head. Soft lighting, innovative displays, cool music, lots of fresh, organic, natural products. A salad and soup bar, for goodness' sake, and seating, so you can eat it right away.

In one of their recent Facebook postings, on a Sunday at 7:47 A.M., WFM asked the simple question: "Good morning, what's for breakfast?" 615 people replied. Some answers were short and sweet, saying "pancakes" and so on. But others showed more love:

> *"Melon and Greek yogurt. All from Whole Foods although I couldn't afford the price and other stores with the same brand are less expensive in today's economy, I went ahead and purchased it. I think it made me feel important to be able to buy from Whole Foods. Still looking for work since 2009. We luv Whole Foods and are looking forward to guilt-free shopping with you."*

So even a customer who is apparently out of work still buys at the more expensive WFM and feels good about it. These types of comments are not unusual on the company's page.

More than 2,000 comments were posted after Mackey wrote a *Wall Street Journal* op-ed piece about the health care reform bill being considered by Washington in 2010. According to the company, WFM pays 100 percent of the residual insurance premiums for full-time team members, almost 90 percent of their workforce. Additionally, those team members get to vote for their new plan options every three years. These policies are widely known, so WFM customers know that they support a company that supports its workers.

In his article, Mackey took a position against the more liberal health care reform that the Obama administration was pushing. But WFM customer comments were mostly supportive:

> *"I am so glad John Mackey spoke up! Thank you! I will shop more at Whole Foods because of it!"*

> *"Jack Mackey has outstanding character! His ideas make complete sense to me! I'm going out of my way to buy from Whole Foods now— even driving out of town to make purchases."*

> *"My wife and I have become Whole Foods customers because of John Mackey's courageous stand of simply sharing his story of what works at Whole Foods. Congratulations, John, for having the guts to buck the mainstream wisdom of many of your customers. Here in St. Louis you have picked up a whole bunch of new customers because of the courage of your convictions!"*

> *"I am a big fan of Whole Foods and what they represent. I, however, am in shock that such a seemingly progressive company opposes health care reform . . ."*

> *"Bravo Mr. Mackey for doing the RESPONSIBLE thing for your employees . . . I only hope that more American companies learn from your excellent example . . ."*

CONCLUSION

It is not easy to make, and keep, customers happy. But as we have seen in this chapter, customer happiness can provide immense value to a business. When customers are content and satisfied, or feel joy when you delight them, they will become not only loyal but also recommend your company and brand to their family, friends and colleagues. They will share their positive views with the world via social media. Thus, it is worthwhile for any company, large or small, to look at how to bring happiness to customers.

In the next chapter, we will examine more closely the concept of happiness and what philosophers and psychologist have found out about the nature of happiness. In the following chapters, I will present three methods for making customers happy. Throughout the book, we will examine how some companies have used these insights to build strong businesses.

2

WHAT CAN POSITIVE PSYCHOLOGY TEACH US?

Happiness is the number-one goal in most people's lives. That's why there are countless books on what makes people happy, or how people can change their circumstances to become more positive and cheerful. But if we believe the many surveys that have been conducted on happiness, very few people have reached that goal. Most people are, to put it mildly, less than happy.

Maybe that's why modern-day companies have begun to take the easy route to instill "happiness" in customers: they use the word "happy" in the company name, brand name or products. It takes no deep customer insight, complex strategy or marketing campaign to use the word "happy" to attract customers. It is by definition the lowest-hanging fruit.

Here is a partial list of those "happy" companies and "happy" brands and products.

We will begin with the *Happy Company*.[1] This company sells lifestyle products in 17 countries and promises in its mission statement "to create unique, high-quality, affordable products that bring you a sense of well-being and provide stress-relieving solutions for the pressures of today's fast-paced world. We want our customers to feel good about them and project vitality in our communities, creating a happier world."

Seattle-based *Happy Thoughts* promises "unforgettable events and gifts without all the stress!" If yesterday wasn't so good, perhaps *Happy New Day Inc.* or *Happy Things* will have what you need.

The *Happy Empire* will sort out your software needs; *Happy Foot* will keep you walking; and *Happy Music* will keep you playing the right tune. To keep your children smiling, try *Happy Kids* or *The Happy Tomato*, an online kid's nontoxic and biodegradable clothing site that sources from global sewing co-ops.

If you're an animal lover, you may find bliss at *Happy Critters Collection, Happy Hounds, Happy Dog Toys, Happy Puppy Kindergarten* or *Happy Goat Farm*. At *Happy Mountain Farm* in Covington, Washington, they offer 20 breeds of miniature cattle.[2] Their motto: "Happy Cows Come from Happy Mountain® Farm." There you can get information about how to buy a mini-cow, as well as order fresh (and "fantastic!") mini-cow steaks online and mini-cow embryos and semen for worldwide export to breeders.

Of course the granddaddy of truly happy companies is *The Happy Cooperative*, a medical marijuana dispensary in Southern California.[3] If you can't get happy there, it may not be possible for you to get happy anywhere! To ensure your happiness, they offer the following "Daily Specials."

- Happy Hour: 4:20 pm until closing every Monday–Friday. 4 Gram Eighths [*sic*], 7.5 Gram Quarters!
- Early Bird Catches the "J." Free Pre-roll w/ $20 donation between 10 am–Noon EVERYDAY!
- Member Ounce Specials: 7 Days a week! Ask your Bud Tender and Look for the "MEMBERS SPECIAL" displays.

I guess I should have expected the website to respond slowly as I was surfing. Perhaps they were all in the backroom of the co-op, testing the merchandise or busy contacting *Happy Joe's Pizza and Ice Cream Parlor, Happy Snacks* or the *Happy Chef* for a delivery of munchies!

While some choose "happy" for the company name, others save it for their products and brands.

If your *Happy Horoscope* suggests it's a good day, take off your *Happy Beginning Clothing* and slip into a bath of *Happy Bath Salts.* After that get onto a *Happy Day Bed* while your *Happy Endings Massage* therapist uses *Happy Massage Oils.* When he or she is done, why not clean up with *Happy Shower Cream, Happy Shower Gel* or *Happy Bubble Bath.* Don't forget to apply *Happy Body Lotion* after you dry off to keep your skin supple. Splash on a bit of Clinique's *Happy Cologne* and you're ready to go.

If you want to cheat on your *Happy Banana Diet,* try a *Happy Hanukkah Chocolate Bar* or some *Happy Trails Mix.* Stepping outside afterward to enjoy your *Happy Days Tobacco* (chewing or smoking), you may notice the green lawn that's taken care of by *Happy Grass Fertilizers* or be in the mood to set up your kid's *Happy Cabana Playpen.* Of course, the little one will want *Happy Day Candy,* a *Happy Teddy* or a *Happy to Be Me Doll* or even a performing *Happiness Clown*. Encourage his or her school studies by putting a *Happiness Pen-Pack* in his or her *Happy Backpack*.

If all of this happy talk is making you less so, just grab a glass of *Happy Frog Wine* or a cup of *Happy Tea* and slip onto the *Happy Sleeper Mattress* in your bedroom decorated with *Happy Hues Paint*. If your dog comes along and starts to bother you while you're trying to relax, toss him a *Happy Dog Toy* and tell him it's time for his *Happy 'N' Healthy Dog Food*.

Increasingly, companies use the "H" word not only for corporate names, or for their products and brands, but also in brand lines and ad slogans. Ben & Jerry's offers a "scoop of happiness." Club Med positions itself as a place "where happiness means the world." Itsu, a UK fast food chain, promises "health and happiness." And Hong Kong casual apparel retailer Bossini states "Be Happy."

Clearly, making your customers truly happy takes more than using the "H" word. Happiness is a much more serious matter. So let's turn to a more serious topic: the history and development of the concept of happiness.

THE HISTORY OF HAPPINESS

In a series of insightful articles and a book titled *Happiness: A History*, professor of history Darrin M. McMahon examined how people have thought about happiness over the centuries.[4] For most of history, though, we do not have access to the voices of ordinary people. There were no surveys or blogs. We don't know how the Greeks, Romans and Chinese of ancient times or the Europeans of the seventeenth, eighteenth and nineteenth centuries thought about happiness. We can only infer their beliefs through the works of spiritual teachers and philosophers such as Buddha and Confucius, Socrates and Cicero, or John Locke and Arthur Schopenhauer. In the absence of other evidence we may also look at language, and that's exactly what Professor McMahon did.

He shows that the concept of happiness, as defined in chapter 1—a prolonged emotional state of contentment or a temporary state of joy—is a relatively recent idea. The idea of happiness as "something that we really ought to have—and, moreover, something that's within our power to bring about, if only we set our minds to it" dates back only to the seventeenth and eighteenth centuries.[5] At that time, the spirit of the Enlightenment ushered in a shift from belief in destiny toward individual choice and responsibility and made "the pursuit of happiness" not only a human right but also a personal responsibility. Prior to the late seventeenth century, happiness was viewed as either predetermined, the product of luck or something for the afterlife, as in Christian conceptions of happiness.

The history of language use of *happiness* supports this view. In almost every Indo-European language, the word for *happiness* is a homonym with the word for *luck*. In my native language, German, the word *Glück* means both happiness and luck. Only modern English is excepted, with its two separate words, "happy" and "lucky," and even there the Old English root for happiness is *hap*, meaning luck or chance.

Thus language reflected the belief that happiness was not something an individual could control; rather, it was something that happened to you. Even in the nineteenth century, some philosophers still espoused this view. Schopenhauer wrote, "The positive and perfect happiness is impossible; you just have to expect a comparatively less painful condition."[6]

This kind of thinking reminds me of the way customers were treated, and how they thought of themselves, during much of the twentieth century. In the early stages of market capitalism, a production orientation prevailed. The focus was not on the consumer, but on the company and its internal operations. Consumers were supposed to take what they got and had little choice. Customer satisfaction, customer delight and customer happiness were of minimal concern. Sadly, in some companies, especially monopolistic markets, this ethos still prevails. But increasingly it is the exception. In the consumer-oriented, experience-focused economy today, customers have the say, and their happiness is a central priority for successful organizations.

In the history of happiness, the ancient Greeks were something of an exception. For them, happiness—or *eudaimonia*—was an important goal in an individual's life, and was not associated with luck. First Socrates and Plato, then Aristotle and the schools of the Stoics taught that happiness could be earned and learned, and was a matter of virtue, of living a moral and ethical life, even though it might include sacrifice or pain. In other words, happiness resulted from doing the right thing, often as part of a community. As Aristotle famously said, "Happiness is a life lived according to virtue."

Living a happy life, by this definition, takes an extraordinary amount of effort, discipline and commitment. Many people will fail. The truly happy will only be, as Aristotle said, the "happy few."

Once again, there is a parallel to our current consumer society. Today, some consumers strive for more than pleasure in consumption. They realize that consumerism alone—being able to afford as many goods as possible—does not make them happy. They want to act and behave responsibly as consumers. They are interested in finding out whether the products and services they buy and the companies that produce them follow value standards. For them, being a happy consumer means finding meaning in what they buy. Like the happy few in Greek culture, at this stage they may be a small segment of the market. For instance, there are select consumers who demand green products; they worry about sustainability; they want organizations to be open and transparent. They may not be the majority yet, but they are vocal, confident and inquisitive, and their worldwide numbers are growing fast.

The seventeenth and eighteenth centuries launched what Professor McMahon calls a "happiness revolution." The French *Encyclopédie,* the bible of the European Enlightenment, declared that every individual has a right to be happy. For Thomas Jefferson, the right to pursue happiness became a self-evident truth, and English philosopher John Locke wrote that the "business of man is to be happy."[7]

Happiness became associated with pleasure—a truly liberating and revolutionary attitude. Pleasure is good. Pain is bad. The goal is to strive for the former and minimize the latter. Happiness is about the little "highs" of pleasure. Pleasurable moments replace a well-lived life as the source of happiness, and *feeling* good replaces *being* good. By associating happiness with pleasure, happiness suddenly becomes much easier to achieve. As such, the consumer society of the late twentieth and early twenty-first centuries would seem to be the perfect environment for achieving happiness. Consumerism provides instant gratification by making available a massive number of products for ordinary consumers. Consumers today seem to experience one happiness moment after another just by immersing themselves in shopping, buying and consuming the never-ending variety of new products and product variations offered to them.

It is precisely this kind of happiness that has become the target of criticism of psychologists like Professor Ed Diener. Referred to as "Mr. Happiness," Diener published hundreds of books and articles on the subject and studied thousands of people across 140 nations, more than anyone else. He created the "Satisfaction with Life" scale, a frequently used tool in happiness research.[8] One of the major tenets of his work is that "materialism is toxic for happiness."[9] He feels that people who are connected with family and friends, who lose themselves in enjoyable daily activities or are not concerned with keeping up with the Joneses, are the happiest people on earth.

Professor McMahon is also critical of the modern concept of happiness. "Don't get me wrong, there is nothing bad about feeling good," McMahon concludes on a critical note.

"But I would suggest that something of value may have been lost or forgotten in our transition to modern ideas of happiness. We can't feel good all the time; nor, I think, should we want to...these are things that the older traditions knew—in the West and the East alike—and that we have forgotten."[10]

ARE YOU HAPPY IN AN ABSOLUTE OR RELATIVE SENSE?

Economists sometimes pose questions in strange ways. For example, they wonder whether people are happy in an *absolute* or *relative* sense, and there are proponents of both views. Let me explain.

Supporters of the absolute view argue that the amount of money one has, and thus the amount of goods consumed, determines happiness. If you have more money, allowing you to acquire and consume more goods, you are happier than someone who has less money and can acquire and consume fewer goods. In contrast, proponents of the relative view argue that happiness is determined in relation to others: it depends on the amount of money and products you can acquire and consume relative to your reference group. Despite extensive research, there is no definitive answer; some studies support the absolute view and others the relative view.

In a 2009 article titled "Wealth, Warmth and Well-Being: Whether Happiness Is Relative or Absolute Depends on Whether It Is About Money, Acquisition, or Consumption," Chris Hsee, a behavioral economist at the University of Chicago, and his co-authors showed that whether you are happy, in an absolute or relative sense, depends on the object of consumption.[11] For what Hsee and his co-researchers call "inherently evaluable variables," that is, variables for which people have an "innate scale"—such as temperature, sleep and orgasms—happiness is absolute. But for what they call "invaluable variables," for which there is no innate measurement, such as jewelry, handbags and cars, happiness is relative. You compare yourself to the neighbors.

To support their theory, Hsee and his co-researchers conducted a large-scale field survey in 31 cities in mainland China, where they measured city dwellers' happiness with their room temperature and their jewelry, for example. Each variable (room temperature and jewelry) included within-city and between-city variations. The study was conducted in the winter: some participants (the rich) could afford warmer room temperatures than others. Reported room temperatures varied from roughly 13.5 degrees Celsius to 21 degrees Celsius (from 56 to 70 degrees Fahrenheit) and thus went from brrrrrr to comfortable. A comparison of the scatter plots of the relation between room temperature and happiness, and jewelry value and happiness, revealed compelling evidence for the theory: Happiness with temperature was absolute, but happiness with jewelry was relative. Being warm makes you happier, period. More jewelry makes you happier only if you have more than your neighbors or the reference group.

The study has implications for how we treat consumers at the "bottom of the pyramid." The influential "bottom of the pyramid" model, introduced by the late strategist C. K. Prahalad, calls on companies not to exclude the poor as consumers, but view them as consumer targets by producing and marketing the products they really want.[12] If Hsee and his co-authors are right, then a few of these products may improve poor consumers' happiness, but many won't. Consumer happiness may not come from the sheer acquisition of goods, but from making products and brands relevant and meaningful to each individual consumer.

In other words, happiness is ultimately about consumer psychology. Let's try to understand happiness from a psychological perspective by exploring some insights of modern psychology.

THE POSITIVE PSYCHOLOGY MOVEMENT

More than 50 years ago, the well-known psychologist Abraham Maslow, in his seminal book *Motivation and Personality*, proposed in the last chapter, titled "Toward a Positive Psychology," that psychologists should focus on personal growth, self-sacrifice, love, optimism, spontaneity, courage, acceptance, contentment, humility, kindness and actualization of psychological potential.[13] However, for the next 50 years, psychology became obsessed with assessing and understanding mental diseases and disorders. Clinical psychologists dedicated their attention to the diagnosis and treatment of pathologies and abnormal behaviors rather than focusing on the positive aspects of life. Social psychology studied biases and errors (including the "positivity bias") of human behavior. Ten years ago, a search of the psychological literature turned up approximately 200,000 published articles on the treatment of mental illness, 80,000 on depression, 65,000 on anxiety, 20,000 on fear, 10,000 on anger and only about 1,000 on positive concepts and human capabilities.[14]

The positive psychology movement changed all that. Since the turn of the millennium, pioneering psychologists like Martin Seligman, Mihaly Csikszentmihalyi, Christopher Peterson, Daniel Gilbert, and others in this field have refocused the spotlight on positive aspects of psychological science—such as happiness. Gilbert has even created an iPhone app with which you can track your happiness and contribute to his research.

The seminal moment for this movement came in 1998, when Seligman gave his presidential address to the American Psychological Association.[15] Seligman called for his colleagues to go back to the roots of psychology and identify what makes for an excellent human life. When Seligman turned his interest to the study of happiness, he had already established himself as a key researcher in the study of depression—or, as he called it, "learned helplessness." He argued that clinical and social psychologists like him had been preoccupied with mental illness and had neglected a whole other realm of psychology.

Because of that 1998 speech and his subsequent work, Martin Seligman is considered the father of the positive psychology movement. He directs the Positive Psychology Center at the University of Pennsylvania's Psychology Department, where scholars are dedicated to studying positive experiences, positive personality traits and positive institutions.

Seligman's view of happiness is broad and multifaceted and has evolved over time. Early on, he wrote about what he called the Pleasant Life, the Good Life and the Meaningful Life. The Pleasant Life is a life characterized by positive emotions about the present, past and future. The Good Life emphasizes individual strengths and virtues. The Meaningful Life uses those strengths and virtues in the service of something larger than oneself. In his latest book, *Flourish: A Visionary New Understanding of Happiness and Well-being,* he talks about four factors that help people thrive and find a multilayered life of well-being: positive emotion, engagement with what one is doing, a sense of accomplishment and good relationships.[16]

Of particular relevance to business and marketing (and thus this book) is a psychological model that he developed together with Christopher Peterson, another psychologist and expert in optimism, health and well-being. Together they argue that people seek life satisfaction via three orientations: (1) Pleasure, (2) Meaning and (3) Engagement. In chapters 3, 4 and 5 I will present methods that companies can use to achieve the three corresponding kinds of customer happiness: pleasure happiness, meaning happiness and engagement happiness.

Let's look more closely at their model. I will refer to it henceforth as the "PME Happiness Model."

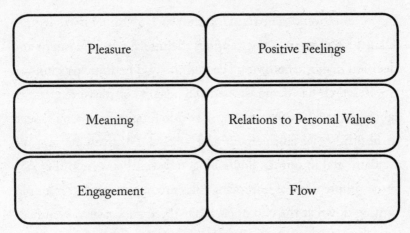

FIGURE 2. THE PME MODEL OF HAPPINESS

THE PME HAPPINESS MODEL

The first orientation of the model—Pleasure—concerns enjoyable and positive experiences. It could also be called the hedonic approach to happiness. The goal is to maximize pleasure and decrease pain. People are naturally happy when they achieve a lot of pleasure with little or no pain.

In the modern world, as we have seen, the pursuit of pleasure is widely viewed as the prime way to achieve happiness: "Don't worry—be happy." But Seligman and Peterson trace the hedonic orientation and concern for immediate gratification all the way back to certain Greek philosophers such as Aristippus (c. 435–366 BCE) and Epicurus (341–270 BCE), Renaissance thinkers such as Desiderius Erasmus (1466–1536) and Thomas More (1478–1535), and the eighteenth-century British philosopher David Hume (1711–1776). More recent explorations of this orientation can be found in the work of Nobel Prize winner Daniel Kahneman, who examines the interface of judgment and decision making, behavioral economics and hedonic psychology.

Research has demonstrated the benefits of pleasure, positive emotions and positive affect on a wide range of outcomes, such as health, social engagement and success. Positive emotions are fundamental to human flourishing and well-being, and there are some simple ways of improving pleasure happiness. For example, writing down at the end of each day three good things that happened can increase happiness. While pleasure and positive affect may not always be ultimately positive (e.g., some pleasures can lead to addictions), there is no question that pleasure and positive emotions are important to well-being.

The second orientation of the PME Happiness Model—Meaning—concerns values and virtues. The goal here is to derive gratification by being true to oneself. A person is happy when he or she successfully identifies values, cultivates them and lives in accordance with them.

The authors traced this orientation to Aristotle's (384–322 BCE) notion of virtue. They also saw traces of this orientation in the philosophical works of John Stuart Mill (1806–1873) and Bertrand Russell (1872–1970) and, in twentieth-century psychology, in Maslow's (1970) concept of self-actualization.

The meaning dimension was also central to the Austrian psychiatrist Victor Emil Frankl (1905–1997). Frankl devoted his life to understanding and promoting the importance of meaning in life. In his most famous book, *Man's Search for Meaning*, he describes how he survived the Holocaust by finding personal meaning in the experience.[17] Subsequently, he developed a form of therapy called logotherapy, focused on the "will to meaning."

Frankl believed that without meaning, people's lives will lead to senseless materialism, boredom and neuroticism. Indeed, his research seemed to indicate a strong relationship between meaninglessness and mental problems, addictions and criminal behavior.

Finally, happiness can also be experienced through an engaged life, which emerges when individuals actively engage in activities that fully immerse them.

The Engagement orientation of the PME Happiness Model is based on the work of Hungarian-born psychologist Mihaly Csikszentmihalyi. He argues that people find genuine happiness during an unusual state of consciousness that he calls "Flow." In the Flow state, individuals are completely absorbed in an activity. Flow may occur when performing a sport or game (e.g., when you ski down a slope or play golf, or when you play a video game or chess). Flow may also occur at work, especially during creative activities. A classical pianist, a Ferrari F1 driver, a trader on Wall Street, even a McDonald's employee who flips hamburgers can experience flow as long as they are fully engaged. During this "optimal experience," individuals are at the peak of their abilities and capabilities. They experience a heightened sense of awareness; they lose track of time and go "into the zone." The mind is entirely absorbed in the activity and action becomes effortless. As Csikszentmihalyi writes, flow is "a state in which people are so involved in an activity that nothing else seems to matter; the experience is so enjoyable that people will continue to do it even at great cost, for the sheer sake of doing it." [18]

Seligman and Peterson have developed an "Orientations to Happiness Questionnaire" to measure these three orientations. Using the scale, they assessed the contributions of each kind of happiness to satisfaction with life. Results indicated that all three kinds predicted satisfaction with life, but Meaning and Engagement were more highly correlated with satisfaction than was Pleasure.

HOW IS THIS MODEL USEFUL FOR BUSINESS?

In chapters 3, 4 and 5, I will build on the PME Happiness Model and show how you can use the three orientations to make your customers happy. I will present one method each to achieve Pleasure, Meaning and Engagement Happiness. I will also show how each method can be used to add pleasure and meaning to customers' lives and to engage them when they shop, buy and consume.

Consumerism and materialism do not have to lead us down a dismal path of unhappiness and despair, as some philosophers and psychologists believe. Companies that are customer-oriented and truly concerned about their customers' happiness can make important contributions to people's lives. Consumers will thank them for it and will reward them with loyalty.

For the remainder of this chapter, let's consider some business examples of how companies can make customers happy by focusing on Pleasure, Meaning and Engagement. We will look at the pleasure of chocolate, the meaning and values provided by a car brand (the Prius) and engagement with a communication software platform (Skype).

THE PLEASURE OF CHOCOLATE

Why does the mere mention of the word "chocolate" give most people a happy feeling? If we believe everything that's been written about it, chocolate can relax you, stimulate you, excite you sexually, help you live a healthier, longer life and even get rid of depression. Chocolate gives us pleasure and inspires our hedonistic selves.

More than 3,000 years ago, the Mayans and Aztecs of Central America were already in love with cocoa beans, using them as a form of money and grinding them into a frothy, beer-like, celebratory chocolate drink. It was apparently bitter and was called *xocolatl,* or "bitter water."[19] Explorers like Columbus and the Spanish conquistadors such as Hernán Cortés who followed him were wowed by the chocolate beverage. While they shattered the Aztec Empire in the sixteenth century, they were smitten enough with the stuff to take it back to Europe. Thus began a long and deep obsession.

Since that discovery, chocolate has morphed from use in sacred ceremonies to medicine to an elixir of love, romance and celebration. Over the last few years in particular, chocolate has become strongly associated with pleasure in the consumer's mind, largely owing to clever and indulgent product design and marketing.

Just look at the industry today—it has garnered an almost fanatical following. From 2008 through 2011 the International Cocoa Organization says that, despite the global financial crisis and recession, global grindings of cocoa beans increased to 3.7 million tons from 3.4 million tons.[20] In their wide-ranging study of chocolate and its special properties, Kristen Morris and Douglas Taren note that the average American eats 4.9 kg of chocolate per year, while per capita sales figures for Switzerland, the highest in the world, are 11.6 kg a year.[21] (Of course, some of this represents purchases by tourists; the average Swiss citizen isn't consuming two 100-g bars of chocolate a week.) American surveys have shown that chocolate cravings represent close to 50 percent of all food cravings. That makes it the most commonly craved food in North America, especially among women.

There is an amazing variety of chocolate in the world. Most people know the international mass-market chocolate brands of Hershey and Cadbury, and of Milka and Lindt. The top ten global confectioners reported sales of USD 67.5 billion in 2010, according to the International Cocoa Organization.[22] But artisanal, high-end chocolate is what gets the true connoisseur hot, bothered and buying.

Sacred Chocolate in San Rafael, California, offers what they call "the world's highest-quality, unroasted (raw), cold-pressed and stone-ground chocolate."[23] Charging USD 30 and more for just a few pieces, they say their products are "handmade with love, gratitude and humility" in a certified organic, vegan, kosher, halal, carbon-balanced factory at a very low temperature to help retain the healthy properties of the bean, including mood-elevating, antidepressant and antioxidant qualities.

To take it up one more luxurious notch, look no further than the Knipschildt Chocolatier of South Norwalk, Connecticut, sellers of one of the most extravagant chocolates in the world.[24] Chef Fritz Knipschildt makes by hand the 1.9 ounce La Madeline au Truffe with "a decadent 70% Valrhona dark chocolate, heavy cream, sugar, truffle oil and vanilla" as the base for the rich ganache. A French Perigord truffle (a rare mushroom) is then surrounded by this rich decadent ganache; it is enrobed in Valrhona dark chocolate and then rolled in fine cocoa powder. The result is pure extravagance, placed on a bed of sugar pearls in a silver box tied with a ribbon. Eat it fast . . . the USD 250 Madeline has only a seven-day shelf life.

Godiva Chocolates may not be quite as expensive as La Madeline au Truffe, but this premium brand has a devout following as well. Started in Belgium in 1926, it has changed hands, belonging to American (Campbell's Soup) and now Turkish (the Ülker Group) owners. It has all sorts of chocolate collections, a chocolate rewards club and an attractive retail presence all around the world.

Women have long been known to harbor special affection for chocolate. Scientists believe women crave more than their fair share owing to their reproductive cycle's need for fat and sugar.[25] Or perhaps hormonal production triggers the chocolate craving. Others believe that a cultural element is at play, whereby women are overwhelmingly targeted in chocolate advertising focusing on romance, love and a little bit of indulgence. Other research has shown that allowing chocolate to melt in your mouth produces brain and heart-rate activity that is similar to that found during passionate kissing. Whatever the reason, if the way to a man's heart is through the stomach, the way to a woman's heart—and wallet—often begins with her sweet tooth.

PRIUS—FINDING MEANING IN A CAR

No one product is more central to the American psyche than the automobile. Wheels are viewed as a birthright and a necessity. Unless Americans are stuck in a traffic jam, they are truly happy when behind the wheel of their machines. But how does the environmentally aware American justify driving an oil- and gasoline-burning behemoth?

Enter the Prius, a car with a new meaning and purpose.

Customers who own a Prius are not only clamoring for the gas savings (45+ mpg), but they also want a product that is environmentally friendly or that at least reduces the impact that a car has on the planet. In other words, they feel happy about burning less fossil fuel. Though the Prius costs more than similar-sized non-hybrids (launched as a compact sedan, the current model has grown into a midsize hatchback for about USD 25,000 in the US), people are happy to pay a bit extra, because they feel that they are making a tangible difference to the world around them.

In fact, the US Environmental Protection Agency (EPA) and California Air Resources Board (CARB) rate the Prius among the cleanest vehicles sold in the United States, based on smog-forming and toxic emissions.[26] With plaudits like that, it is not surprising that by September 2011, more than two million of the cars had been sold worldwide, one million in the US alone. That's a lot of happy customers finding meaning on four wheels!

A Prius chic movement in Los Angeles prompted Hollywood industry people to flock to the car. The Prius became "Hollywood's latest politically correct status symbol."[27] Celebrities like Billy Joel, Brad Pitt, Cameron Diaz, Ewan McGregor, Jack Nicholson, Leonardo DiCaprio, Harrison Ford, Susan Sarandon, Salma Hayek and even Prince Charles all have reportedly taken to driving the gas-sipper.[28] Though the car was popular with left-wing liberal environmentalists from the start, there were also people on the right, dubbed "Prius Patriots," jumping on the hybrid bandwagon.

Finding meaning can take different forms for different people—even in the same product. The former Central Intelligence Agency chief and famous hawk James Woolsey, Jr. says he drives a Prius because using less oil means fewer oil profits go to Middle Eastern regimes, where they might end up in the hands of radical Islamists.[29] He says it's a patriotic obligation to drive more efficient cars.

Prius marketing reinforces consumer perceptions. For example, one ad places the car in a forest and boasts that the car has been "honored by the United Nations, the Sierra Club and the National Nightlife Federation."

Interestingly, data from CNW Marketing Research in 2006–2007 found that 57 percent of Prius buyers admitted to buying the hybrid mostly because "it makes a statement about me," while just 36 percent cited fuel economy as a prime motivator. So while some consumers find meaning through doing what they believe is the "right thing," others may just want people to think that they care about the environment. Luckily, the environment doesn't care which it is!

ENGAGING WITH SKYPE

The Skype software platform was launched in 2003, letting users call and video chat over the Internet. Calls to other users within the Skype service are free, while calls to traditional landline telephones and mobile phones can be made for a small fee.

Skype has become a very popular tool for both business and private usage. Perhaps you are among the 600 million+ connected users (as of fall 2011) of Skype.[30]

But Skype is not just about calls. It engages the user with various features, including instant messaging, file transfer and video conferencing. You can easily get hooked on Skype, using it for all your communication needs and, as business users, for your team. Plus, they are inventing new features all the time. Those new features are communicated and promoted directly when you sign in to use Skype, which most users do automatically when booting up their computer, smartphone or tablet.

Skype has made massive changes in how we communicate for both business and leisure. It has entered the vernacular in verb form as a synonym for video and voice communications: "Want to Skype?" or "Let's Skype before the kids go to bed" when mom or dad is on a business trip.

Other companies, like Microsoft and Apple, actually had functional video conferencing software before Niklas Zennström and Janus Friis, the founders of the Luxembourg-based Skype, broke through to the masses by offering this unique, useful, free, cool service.

In fact, Microsoft clearly recognizes the transformational properties of Skype: In May 2011, Microsoft agreed to buy its parent company for USD 8.5 billion, acquiring all Skype technologies.[31] That's the ultimate salute to a good product and strong brand. According to the official Microsoft press release, the acquisition of Skype will "increase the accessibility of real-time video and voice communications, bringing benefits to both consumers and enterprise users and generating significant new business and revenue opportunities."[32]

But there's serious competition knocking at the door.[33] Google is promising a fight with its free social networking platform, Google+. Among its many initial unique functions, Google+ enables up to ten-person video conferencing and shares content on screens in a social networking format. "Hangouts," as this service is called, is generating serious buzz and concern for Skype. In fact, Google+ seems to be making both Microsoft and Facebook nervous—so much so that they have incorporated a Skype video icon on chat boxes, thus leveraging

Microsoft's 1.6 percent stake in Facebook. This allows Facebook users to easily connect by video with friends while on their Facebook page. The old adage "adapt or die" seems to be taking a new twist: "adapt and make your customers as happy as you possibly can."

While it is still too early to tell what impact Google+ will have on Skype and Facebook spaces, it is clear that any market leader needs to be on the lookout for hungry companies engaging their customers and trying to steal them away. Remember the BlackBerry brand in the early days? It was untouchable. Then the iPhone came along. Now a range of very aggressive Android-powered phones from the likes of Samsung and HTC are making waves and offering customers a new, useful and engaging experience. Stay tuned to see how the Google+-Skype-Facebook saga plays out, or which upstart company will enter the field and become the next customer-happiness leader.

DO DIFFERENT CONSUMERS PREFER DIFFERENT KINDS OF HAPPINESS?

Are certain consumers prone to certain kinds of happiness? For example, do certain personality types seek out or respond particularly well to the small pleasurable moments, others to meaning and still others to engagement? The answer to this question may be found in personality psychology, the field that addresses individual differences among people.

The most prominent model to describe human personality in all its facets is the so-called Big Five Factor Model (FFM). The FFM uses broad trait dimensions to describe human personality. If you are interested in your personality type or how you score on each dimension, take a personality test; there are several. The most comprehensive one has 240 items and takes 45 minutes to complete. Others are a bit shorter, but still far too long to be useful for conducting, say, a study with consumers on the Internet. Fortunately, there is one short test that measures each dimension with just two items; it is reliable and valid enough, from a psychometric perspective, to be used with confidence.[34]

Here's the test: write a number (from 1 to 7) next to each statement to indicate the extent to which you agree or disagree with that statement. Use a "1" if you strongly disagree, and a "7" if you strongly agree, and the numbers in between for the corresponding levels of agreement. You should rate the extent to which the *pair* of traits applies to you, even if one characteristic applies more strongly than the other.

I see myself as:

1. _____ Extroverted, enthusiastic.
2. _____ Critical, quarrelsome.
3. _____ Dependable, self-disciplined.
4. _____ Anxious, easily upset.
5. _____ Open to new experiences, complex.
6. _____ Reserved, quiet.
7. _____ Sympathetic, warm.
8. _____ Disorganized, careless.
9. _____ Calm, emotionally stable.
10. _____ Conventional, uncreative.

Now score yourself according to the scoring sheet at the end of this chapter.

The Big Five are:

- **Openness**—Being open to new experiences, inventive, curious. People who score high in this trait appreciate the arts, are creative and seek a variety of experiences.
- **Conscientiousness**—Being self-disciplined, organized and efficient. People who score high on this trait plan their behavior rather than being spontaneous in an easygoing way.
- **Extroversion**—Being outgoing, energetic and emotional, especially in the presence of others. People who score high on this trait seek stimulation; they like to be with others and are not reserved.
- **Agreeableness**—Being sympathetic, friendly, kind. People who score high on this trait are compassionate and cooperative rather than critical or suspicious.
- **Emotional Stability**—Being calm, rather than anxious or easily upset. People who score high on this trait show few unpleasant emotions or neurotic symptoms such as anger, anxiety or depression.

Note that, from a positive psychology perspective, each of these dimensions can contribute to well-being and a good life; one is not better than another. But people usually place higher value on some than on others.

So which type is most likely to experience happiness based on pleasurable moments? Look at the descriptions above for each dimension again; intuitively, openness seems to be the answer, and research has confirmed this. Individuals high in openness make remote and unusual associations; they are curious, innovative and imaginative. Open people notice more about the world. They experience more pleasure at the sound of crackling wood in the fireplace or the sound of rain.[35] They get chills when they encounter beautiful music or great art.[36]

As a result, they also notice the little details that you use to enrich their experience with your products. They will be more likely to savor these experiences. When you expand your business, they will notice and approve.

Conscientious personalities, on the other hand, are more likely to experience meaning happiness, and extroverted personalities are more likely to experience engagement happiness.

PLEASURE + MEANING + ENGAGEMENT

Through positive psychology, we have learned that there are three distinct ways to make customers happy: pleasure, meaning and engagement. Thus far, we have treated each orientation separately. However, these three concepts are intricately linked. Marketers often use at least two, if not all three, to make their customers happy.

Consider the marketing of life insurance—specifically, Prudential's recent campaign. The Prestige Customer Program is designed for their high-net-worth customers. The entry on their website looks like a commercial for the pleasurable life: a tuxedo-clad man drinks champagne, a woman gets a massage and a couple enjoys a big glass of red wine.[37] Next to the pictures are corresponding phrases: "For the distinguished few who enjoy life's finest . . . Savour the finest . . . Enjoy priority services . . . Specially brought to you by Prudential." What it doesn't say is, "Buy a life insurance policy so that when you die, your loved ones will get some cash." This is about being happy and enjoying life now.

But Prudential also talks about meaning and values. The thrust of its communications is that Prudential wants to build wealth for loved ones by reminding them of their responsibility to provide and plan for their family. The website shows, for example, a grandfather playing with his grandson, apparently "enjoy[ing] lifelong protection." Another spot shows a father and a son relaxing on a park bench. There customers read, "Your gift of love. Your legacy of protection." The thought of giving love to and leaving a legacy of protection for family will undoubtedly resonate with current or potential customers.

"I don't think people want to think about death," said Ken Kim, director of Brand Communications at Prudential Financial in an interview for this book. "People want to think about living their lives, which is why talking about retirement is a more interesting conversation to have with an agent or financial advisor. You're going to think about what you're going to be doing with your money that you've saved up over your working years. I do think that the act of purchasing life insurance can provide a happy feeling once someone ultimately decides to do so."[38]

Similarly, think back to Godiva. To be sure, as with any chocolate manufacturer, pleasure is a major focus of their campaign. But Godiva is also increasingly focused on engaging its customers. Since 2008, their chocolates have been available to customers via four sales channels: retail stores, catalog, the Internet and a mobile app.[39] They thus engage their customers in a variety of ways, which, for a chocoholic, is very good news. Godiva also draws its customers closer through its Rewards Club. To those who sign up on their website they offer several benefits:[40]

- A free piece of chocolate every month
- A free gift each month that the customer spends USD 10 or more
- Free standard shipping for one online order
- Online special offers every month

Additionally, via the website and mobile app, customers can easily buy and send their favorites to family, friends or colleagues. As the mobile site says, "It's the perfect way to send a thoughtful gift when you're on the run. Godiva Mobile brings the experience of Godiva.com to the palm of your hand."[41]

CONCLUSION

So far, we have presented the business case for customer happiness and explored useful concepts from philosophy and psychology. We have seen that turning customers into happy customers can provide immense value to a company. We have also seen that there are several pertinent and underutilized concepts in positive psychology for making customers happy.

In the next three chapters, I will show you how the concepts of pleasure, meaning and engagement can help you develop practical approaches and implementations in the quest for customer happiness.

SCORING SHEET FOR
PERSONALITY TEST (PAGE 48)

1. Reversely code items 2, 4, 6, 8 and 10. That is, a 1 becomes a 7, a 2 becomes a 6, and a 3 becomes a 5.

2. Add up items 5 and 10 for your final score for "openness"; items 3 and 8 for "conscientiousness"; items 1 and 6 for "extroversion"; items 2 and 7 for "agreeableness"; and items 4 and 9 for "emotional stability."

3

THE "FEEL GOOD" METHOD

The "Feel Good" method creates pleasurable moments that can be the starting point of a customer relationship. As we will see, the method enriches the customer experience and gets customers to pay attention to the details of the experience. W Hotels offers a great example.

W HOTELS

Mention W Hotels, and most people picture trendy customers sitting around a swank lobby bar. The brand has cultivated an image suggesting that you might see cool designers, rock stars or perhaps the latest artist mingling with the hip staff. Defining their niche this way, W properties ensure buzz, and in many cities they've become *the* place to be.

W was never supposed to be an average hotel for tourists or business people. Serious business people, depending on their expense account, would stay at the Four Seasons, Ritz-Carlton,

Sheraton, Westin, Hilton, Marriott or any number of other places where the service is good, perhaps even exceptionally good. But honestly, none of those properties exudes "cool."

Most of the standard hotels have efficient check-in, a club floor and lounge, fitness facilities, decent restaurants, room service and turn-down service with a piece of chocolate on your pillow. But, traditionally, hotels have not so much been about the customer as they have been about selling out rooms and guaranteeing turnover: Check 'em in and check 'em out.

Along came W in 1998 and it totally redesigned the hotel experience. They changed the formula, the notion of what it means to stay at a hotel. All of sudden, a chain hotel was a fun, trendy and happy place to be. They made it a lifestyle destination where there was always a party (or at least the promise of one), where one could find chic decor, a great bar with interesting, beautiful people and a DJ spinning new music. There's a Bliss Spa to help unwind from a stressful day, Sweat Fitness to burn some calories, and a signature restaurant (chefs Drew Nieporent, Todd English and Tom Colicchio are some of their collaborators) where trendy, delicious food draws both staying guests and locals in the know.[1] W professes to take a "strikingly modern approach to design that is as refreshing, accessible and comfortable as one's own living space [with] an emphasis on comfort, warmth, attentive service and exceptional amenities."[2]

In short, the W experience is about feeling good, and it is entirely about you, the experience-craving customer.

One of their signature services is the Whatever/Whenever, one-stop 24/7 concierge to keep customers happy. They describe it on their website:

"Birthday Party at 35,000 Feet? Wedding Dress Pickup by Helicopter? Bathtub of Hot Chocolate? At W Hotels, your wish is truly our command with our Whatever/Whenever® service. We'll make your special moment magical, and transform your dreams into reality. Whatever you want. Whenever you want (as long as it's legal!)."[3]

It's not clear how many hot chocolate-filled bath tubs have been requested since the first W at 49th Street and Lexington Avenue opened in New York City, but the concept immediately struck a chord with people who wanted quality in a chic setting. Within two years, more than a dozen W properties dotted the US, from Chicago to Atlanta, New Orleans to Los Angeles, San Francisco, Seattle and Honolulu. Once the haunt of media players on the West Coast and sophisticated urbanites seeking a balance between style and substance, the chain has now moved toward the mainstream. It markets to discerning people (including business people) who desire a bit of an edge during their stay, an upscale romantic getaway, or even a family vacation. Now there are nearly 40 locations in major cities worldwide, and W Resorts in vacation spots like Bali, the Maldives and Koh Samui, Thailand.

By all accounts, within the next few years, there will be many more of them. Between now and 2015, W properties are planned for Mexico City, the Riviera Maya, Cairo, Paris, Milan, Athens, St. Petersburg, Abu Dhabi, Shanghai and Beijing. One of the coolest will likely be W Mumbai, which is expected to be in a mixed-use development called "Namaste Tower," whose shape reflects the Namaste yoga gesture—two wings of the hotel are clasped together like hands in meditation.

I have stayed in many W Hotels over the years—Los Angeles, San Francisco and Chicago; in Seoul and Taipei; and even in New York, where I live. I love that some are ultrabright and others brutally dark. I love their approach to food—fresh, local, fun. I love the bars that are always hopping and the Bliss Spas. I took participants in my experience executive programs in New York City to W Times Square. Each time I do research with colleagues at UCLA, I stay at W Westwood. I love the little pool where you can barely get your feet wet but can look so fashionable with a blueberry martini in your hand. I love the banner there that states, "Worldwide Wow. Now." After several years of staying at W, I still smile when I hear "Whatever/Whenever."

In sum, I love the innovative little bits that put me in a good mood and give me small, joyful, happy moments. Those moments may be fleeting, but so what? That's what W is all about: an easygoing, playful approach and the joy and pleasure of the moment.

One of the ironies, of course, is that the W parent company is anything but a small, edgy hotelier. Starwood Hotels and Resorts also own Sheraton, Westin, St. Regis and Le Méridien among others. W Hotels was developed internally by Starwood under the helm of former founder and CEO Barry Sternlicht, a hotelier with vision. It was not acquired.

Starwood is very protective of the W brand and its identity. In 2008, it charged two former Starwood executives, who had joined Hilton's hotel development team, with stealing documents to help Hilton develop its own version of W Hotels named "Denizen." This started an unusually nasty feud that pitted the two hotel giants against each other. In December 2010, the case ended in a settlement. Hilton agreed to pay USD 75 million to Starwood, and was banned until January 2013 from developing a hotel brand that would compete in the same category as the W Hotel chain. Moreover, to supervise Hilton's compliance with a permanent injunction entered in the *Starwood v. Hilton* litigation, the court appointed a branding/marketing monitor to oversee their cooperation with certain branding and marketing provisions.[4]

Of course, some imply that W Hotel itself is a knock-off. Ian Schrager, an American hotelier and real estate developer, once said that "there isn't an idea in W that's original." Schrager was the co-founder of Studio 54, the legendary nightclub in the 1970s and '80s in Manhattan.[5] He subsequently started the Morgan Hotel Group, which includes the Royalton, Paramount and Hudson in New York, the Mondrian in Los Angeles, and the Sanderson and St. Martin's Lane in London, and defined the boutique hotel category.

After W's stunning success in recent years, they are now playing around with their formula. Sensing a market for less-expensive lodging, where design is cool but service is limited, Starwood Hotels and Resorts started a sub-brand in 2008 called Aloft. Seventy-eight of these hotels are currently open around the world (as of fall 2011) and another 30 are expected to be completed by 2014. At less than USD 200 per night, it's much more affordable than, say, W on Lexington in New York City where rates can easily top USD 400 per night. The Aloft motto is "style at a steal."

The first Aloft opened in the Montreal airport in 2008, and the chain quickly spread through the US, Asia, Europe and South America. Aimed at 20- and 30-somethings, they are all super-chic and blindingly colorful; many are near airports. They have pod chairs in the lobby, along with a pool table and the signature w xyz bar; all encourage hanging out. The staff dresses in polo shirts; one blogger described the vibe as "being in a fraternity house." (To be fair, that person admitted to being 40-something and was likely not the target market.)

Technology plays a big part in the customer experience. Radio frequency identification cards (RFID) serve as room keys at many of the properties.[6] If you join their "smart check-in" program in advance, they'll text you your room number on check-in day; just use your Aloft Starwood card with embedded chip to automatically open the room door. No need to stop at the front desk. It's very cutting-edge and exactly what the demographic wants: serve me, make it easy for me, make it look cool and make sure everything works, and I'll savor the experience—without the external stuff, like standing in a check-in line, to ruin it.

Moreover, all the rooms have 42-inch LCD TVs, along with lots of plugs and laptop hookups. Other features may be slightly surprising for an older traveler: The shower has a frosted glass wall looking into the bedroom, offering a partial view of whoever's showering. As at W properties, there are Bliss toiletries in the bathrooms.

What you won't find are trendy restaurants, bathtubs, big closets, a Bliss Spa. There's no room service at Aloft, but a 24-hour pantry in the lobby called re:fuel charges for cappuccinos, cupcakes, deli sandwiches, fresh fruit and the like. These omissions keep room rates lower, allowing younger, less-wealthy clients to savor the W experience without breaking the bank on stuff they probably won't need or use. Aloft may turn out to be a "gateway hotel" in that, if these younger clients are happy with the brand at an early age, they may graduate to W Hotels later in life.

The idea of creating pleasure for Aloft customers is straightforward, but is differently executed than at W Hotels. At W, it's all about asking for what you want, Whatever/Whenever. At Aloft, it's about offering a community if you want it. Both brands offer innovative and contemporary hotel experiences with lots of pleasure happiness.

THE PROBLEMS OF PLEASURE— AND THE SOLUTION

Pleasure and joy are arousing and exciting dimensions of human experience. Pleasure is often associated with the hedonistic aspects of life, like eating or sex. Remember Sigmund Freud's "pleasure principle"? He stipulated that pleasure is an expression of the *id,* the impulsive side of the human psyche.

One potential problem with pleasure-induced happiness is that it does not last. It is transient. That's why many philosophers in the past felt that pleasure happiness should be avoided—because it is superficial and deceiving.

In fact, pleasure seeking and the feelings resulting from pleasure have been associated with addiction or compulsion. Just like an alcohol or drug addict or a compulsive gambler, shopping hedonists cannot control themselves. Thus, a fashionista is not just a devoted follower of fashion; she (or he) is really a shopping addict, always in search of a new rush, of the latest Chanel, Dior or Prada outfit. The techno-geek who needs to replace his (or her) smartphone or PDA every few months is not just involved in the category; that person is addicted to having the latest and greatest. Even a foodie doesn't just have refined taste. Foodies are addicted to discovering more and more unusual ingredients or restaurants.

Indeed, shopaholicsanonymous.org lists the following causes of compulsive shopping and similar consumption disorders:

- Emotional deprivation in childhood
- Inability to tolerate negative feelings
- Need to fill an inner void
- Need to seek excitement
- Need to seek approval
- Perfectionism
- Genuine impulsiveness and compulsiveness
- Need to gain control

This list sounds serious!

In a less pathological way, pleasure happiness has been compared to a "hedonic treadmill." For instance, why do individuals report relatively unstable levels of happiness even when they have higher incomes and buy and consume more? In chapter 2, we said that this is because happiness is relative. Another explanation may be that people quickly adapt to a new situation; new positive events do not raise their level of happiness, at least not in the long term. The pursuit of happiness is thus compared to a person on a treadmill who must work harder and harder just to stay in the same place. You must shop more and more to get the same rush; you must get the latest gadget sooner than others; you must eat better and better food—just to stay on the level.

Do we really have to compare shopping and consuming, even at extreme levels, to an addiction? Is there no way off the hedonic treadmill? Or is there a way to shop and consume *responsibly?*

I believe that shopping and consuming do not have to be superficial and addictive. They can be psychologically rewarding and meaningful for individuals. They can involve perceptual differentiation and learning—higher-order cognitions—rather than just impulsive behavior.

This argument is consistent with recent neuropsychological studies. Early research, conducted in the 1950s by two psychologists at McGill University, James Olds and Peter Milner, suggested that there is one single pleasure center and that pleasure is addictive: rats fanatically pressed levers (up to 2,000 times per hour) to receive tiny pleasurable jolts of current to electrodes inserted in this pleasure center. Other research identified dopamine as the key pleasure chemical. However, modern research shows that things are far more complicated. In a Johns Hopkins Discovery Medicine article titled the "Functional Neuroanatomy of Pleasure and Happiness," two neuroscientist experts, Morten Kringelbach of the University of Oxford and Kent Berridge of the University of Michigan, have reviewed the neuroscientific evidence and concluded that cognitive reflections and learning play a key role in pleasure happiness.[7]

Thus, companies should use a multipronged approach to pleasure happiness, one that provides customers with new discoveries and creative experiences while shopping for Chanel or Dior, when checking out a new smartphone, or when comparing the antioxidant properties of acai versus pomegranate.

EXPERIENCING JOY AND HAPPINESS AT BMW WELT

Joy is the brand core of BMW, and "sheer driving pleasure" is the brand's key communication message. "We make joy" was the title of a 2009 global print campaign, and in the US, the pleasure aspect of the brand is captured in the advertising slogan "The Ultimate Driving Machine."

A major source of pleasure is, of course, the car itself—how it feels on the road, how it performs when accelerating and how well it drives on a curve. For car enthusiasts, this experience is exhilarating, but there is also pleasure in learning the sensory and aesthetic details of the car (the shape of the fenders or sound of a closing door) or new technological features (the pleasure of night vision).

Most important, the joy and pleasure experience can be extended beyond the use of the car itself. BMW Welt (World) is a multifunctional customer experience space in Munich adjacent to the BMW Headquarters, BMW Museum and one of its factories. It was designed by the internationally renowned design firm Coop Himmelb(l)au and opened in 2007. The spectacular architecture expresses the dynamism and excitement of the BMW brand.

BMW Welt provides many value-added activities for current and potential BMW customers and visitors. For example, there are a variety of entertaining events (music and cultural events and movie launches), product demonstrations and food services. There is a lot of interaction between visitors and BMW staff. There is an exciting "staged experience" when customers pick up their vehicle at BMW Welt: they wait for their car on a grand stage as it ascends on a rotating platform and is handed over to the proud owner. Customers from the US and other overseas countries can also come here to collect their car and drive it throughout Europe for a week, then drop it off at a BMW dealership and ship it home. Younger visitors to BMW Welt can educate themselves about car technology in a Junior Camp. Exhibitions and displays change frequently so that customers will want to return, perhaps several times. Management is currently working on all sorts of enhanced tourist packages, membership reward programs and augmented reality views of cars and other displays. In sum, customers and visitors get a close insider look into all aspects of the BMW brand.

When it opened, BMW Welt expected 800,000 visitors per year. In 2010, there were 1.9 million visitors, and there were more than 2 million in 2011. At times, up to 20,000 people visit in just one day, and nearly 50 percent make a return trip. BMW Welt has not only become a destination for car enthusiasts but a tourist destination within the city of Munich.

"BMW Welt is the heart of the brand and the pulse of the city," Manfred Swoboda, who manages guest services at BMW Welt, told me. "We have one common goal here: making customers, guests and visitors happy."

As long as a company can provide such experiences for customers, they will be happy with the company, not in an addictive sense, but in a psychologically complex and deeply rewarding sense. That way, single moments can be extended and customers can experience pleasure and joy many times.

How can we get customers to experience this kind of pleasure happiness? Let's look at the "Feel Good" method.

THE THREE STEPS OF THE "FEEL GOOD" METHOD

The method consists of three interrelated steps: first, enriching the experience for the customer; second, getting the customer to savor the experience and, finally, expanding the experience.

The first step, *Enriching,* requires you to think about the details of the experience you provide to customers. It is about managing design cues. Using this approach, you take a deep dive into the customer's world and design a rich and complex experience for them with multiple connection points that result in small, pleasurable moments.

The next step, *Savoring,* requires that customers notice and focus on the experience that you've designed for them. Savoring is about letting customers do the work, letting them add mentally to what you have created for them in order to make their experience personally relevant.

Finally, *Expanding* means creating new, pleasurable experiences. Expanding is about innovation: new ways for customers to experience your offer—through partnerships, through new channels or through offer extensions. Of course, these expansions can also prolong their savoring of the experience.

The three steps build on each other and overlap. Let's see how each step of the "Feel Good" method can be employed successfully.

STEP 1: ENRICHING

Enriching the experience means making it more positive and pleasurable by increasing the number of touchpoints, providing more details and appealing to the senses. The W case at the beginning of this chapter showed us how to enrich a conventional hotel experience.

To begin with, at W Hotels, there is more to experience than in your ordinary hotel—simply more contact points with the customer. Yes, there is the usual fitness center, but there is also the Bliss Spa where you can pamper yourself. Yes, there is a bar, but

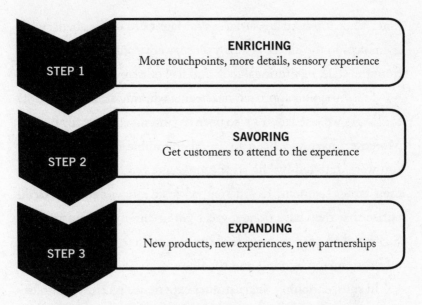

FIGURE 3. THREE STEPS OF THE "FEEL GOOD" METHOD

also a cool lounge next to it. Not only is there beer in your room fridge, but there's a hangover first-aid kit for the morning after, in case you've "lounged" a bit too much.

Moreover, each part of the experience is richer and more detailed. The dining experience may include the hotel classics (the burger, ham and cheese sandwich and some spaghetti dish), but each dish is tweaked to fit modern, healthy lifestyles. The elevator is not just an elevator; it's an experience. At W Westwood in Los Angeles, the camera and display installed in the elevator asks you to "strike a pose" for a real L.A. moment. The check-in staff isn't merely staff; they are responsive people you can engage in intelligent conversation.

Finally, the experience is sensory, and thus easy to remember. W's are design-oriented; there is something visual to be noticed everywhere. There are sounds and music, and I don't mean the usual hotel Muzak. There are surfaces and fabrics to be touched, subtle fragrances in the air. W is a rich sensory environment far removed from the stale, institutional look and feel of many hotel chains.

The enriching approach has been a winning strategy not only for W. As we just saw, it's also been a winning strategy for BMW. Moreover, have you been to an Abercrombie & Fitch store? If you were deterred by the strong fragrance, you are probably not their target segment. If you stepped inside, however, you would notice that they have done a great job of enriching a normal casual retail shopping experience with oversized posters, trendy music, dramatic lighting and the like.

In sum, enriching the customer experience is critical for pleasure happiness. By simply increasing contact points, you increase the probability that customers will have a pleasurable experience and happy moments. By adding detail to each contact point, you intrigue and even surprise customers. By offering concrete and sensory experiences, you attract their attention and gain the opportunity to delight them.

Providing customers with rich experiences, however, is not enough. Sure, getting their attention and exciting their senses may lead to delight and happiness. But you win with your customers if you can get them to savor the experience and become more deeply involved in the experience. Let's look at how this can be done.

STEP 2: SAVORING

Psychologists Fred B. Bryant and Joseph Veroff, co-authors of *Savoring: A New Model of Positive Experience,* have defined "savoring" as "the capacity to attend to, appreciate, and enhance the positive experiences in one's life."[8] Savoring is one of the key positive-psychology strategies to increase well-being, life satisfaction and happiness.

Psychological research has identified many savoring strategies for life happiness. In their book, Bryant and Veroff alone list ten strategies. Sometimes, the advice can get very specific. For example, at www.howtosavor.com, where an anonymous "impatient multi-tasker learns to savor," I found the following blog entry on November 22, 2010:

> *"My husband and I went grocery shopping last night and had a great time. Based on these Nielsen stats, only 14% of consumers in the US really enjoy shopping. People love to talk about why they hate grocery shopping. There is plenty of advice on how to check out during shopping to avoid the pain. Shopping with a partner seems to be especially boring. But we actually loved it."*

They loved the grocery trip because they employed several shopping savoring strategies, including:

> *"We went shopping when and where there were few other people around."*
>
> *"We did not have a list (except for the pantry staples)."*
>
> *"We looked forward to finding new foodstuffs."*
>
> *"We goofed around. For example, I ride the shopping cart while my husband ferries me around."*

So, consumers can be quite inventive when creating their own pleasurable experiences. And firms that listen to such consumers and text-mine their blogs will find plenty of new ideas to improve their business. Indeed, some innovative supermarket retailers worldwide have done exactly that and offer an experience that is very different from the usual drag; shopping at these enlightened places can be exciting and fun.

In chapter 1, I discussed the Whole Foods Market experience. Trader Joe's is another innovative food retailer. It is exactly one of those places where you may go without a shopping list, find new food and even goof around, perhaps with other customers! You may savor every single moment and walk out a little bit happier.

So, it is important to listen to customers' feedback. But there are also three more general ways of getting customers to savor their positive experiences. They are discussed in the positive psychology literature, and I'll apply them here in the business context.

First, make sure the customer is mindful during the experience. Mindful is not the same as being attentive in a rational and analytical way. It means that the customer is not on autopilot but is deliberately directing and focusing attention on the present, pleasant moment—turning a daily routine, like shaving, into a ritual.

Second, get customers to savor the positive experience again, for example, by sharing it with their friends and colleagues. You want them to communicate—indeed celebrate—their positive experience with others.

Finally, customers need to engage in MTT, which in positive psychology means "mental time travel." You want them to vividly remember positive emotions and eagerly anticipate new pleasurable moments.

How this can be accomplished? We can learn a lot from the Japanese. They have turned something as simple as having a bowl of soba noodles into a savoring experience. Soba noodles are buckwheat noodles, ideally made fresh from a stone mill. Here is what I was told in Japan about how to savor a simple bowl of boiled soba:

> *"First, take some time to enjoy its color, shape and presentation. Next, enjoy its fragrance. Then pick up a strand of noodle and eat it plain. This is the best way to taste the natural goodness of fresh soba. Hold the chopsticks in one hand and pick up a bite-sized portion of soba. Finally, dip it in the sauce and slurp the noodles up all at once."*

The slurping is of course a lot of fun. But notice the prior steps, where almost nothing seems to happen. Try it yourself, perhaps with a bowl of spaghetti with olive oil. Or, if you are a coffee drinker, savor your espresso. Illy, the Italian coffee firm, offers instructions on its website (www.illy.com) on how to celebrate the espresso ritual (described as "a momentary pleasure that lingers on"), prepare a perfect espresso (defined as "the quintessential way to enjoy coffee"), and taste it properly (referred to as "a journey through the senses").[9] Savoring is about paying attention to the details of an act that you may have performed many times in order to appreciate it as if it were the first time. Of course, this works best if you MTT the experience and share it with others and talk about it. That way you will also remember it and look forward to experiencing it again in the near future.

Getting customers to savor their experience—by being mindful of the experience, sharing it with others and remembering or anticipating it—is key for pleasure happiness. Savoring deepens the customer experience because it involves a person mentally and emotionally.

STEP 3: EXPANDING

Once you've enriched the experience and succeeded in getting the customer to savor it, you must expand the experience for your customer. Expanding the experience is key because your business likely involves only one aspect of people's lives. If you are the maker of a fruit juice, you only touch customer's lives when they are thirsty and interested in drinking juice. You will be relevant to that customer for only seconds or maybe a couple of minutes. You may enrich that moment for them through antioxidant ingredients and a funky name and packaging, and get them to savor that moment when the cold drink travels down their throat. But let's face it, the experience is limited. Their happiness moments will be short. They may remember it pleasantly and anticipate the next moment, but it would be far better if you could expand beyond that. Wouldn't it be great, for you and your customers, if you could touch their lives more broadly and make them happy beyond the sip of the juice—for example, by offering them not just fruit juice but refreshment more generally and offering that refreshment at various relevant moments and in extended form?

You can achieve this expansion by extending product lines, by offering the experience in new channels, and by teaming up with others through partnerships.

Various companies have done this quite successfully. For example, Apple has expanded its product line drastically over the last ten years, introducing revolutionary products and services like the iPod, iTunes, iPhone and the iPad, thus expanding the user-friendly and cool Apple experience into new products. Google has expanded its business into mobile phones, bringing its search platform into a new channel. Banks are linking up with mobile phone companies to provide more convenient payment options. Paying a bill via a mobile phone can be a real pleasure. No waiting in lines, no going online. All of this feels good to customers.

In sum, through product line extension, new channels and partnerships, you can add more pleasurable moments for customers. If they savor these new experiences as much as the enriched original experience, you are well on your way to delivering pleasure happiness through your brand.

We have discussed the three steps of the "Feel Good" method for making customers happy, so let's look at business cases of companies that make their customers feel good and thus illustrate this method.

"FEEL GOOD" COMPANIES

THE COMMUNAL TABLE AT LE PAIN QUOTIDIEN

Le Pain Quotidien is a franchise chain that Alain Courmont founded in Belgium in 1990. Twenty years later, Le Pain Quotidien has expanded its business into approximately twenty countries, from Australia and Kuwait to Russia and the UK, and has become an international brand. In the US, it has a strong presence in New York and Los Angeles. Le Pain Quotidien offers an enriched experience for customers to savor, and this experience has been expanded over the years.

Courmont started with the idea of baking sourdough wheat bread in the form of 2kg round loaves and selling them in a store. The bread would be eaten with olive oil or marmalade, for example. The store also sold a few other staples of French baking culture: baguettes, croissants, madeleines and café au lait to go with the baked goods.

The logo depicts a loaf of bread pulled from an oven. The website greets its visitors enthusiastically with the phrase "Welcome to our bakery and communal table."[10] The website and Facebook also offer a lesson on how to pronounce the brand name ("luh pan koh-ti-dyaN").

From the start, the concept was enriched by the so-called communal table and its associated elements. Customers can gather around a large table like one you'd find in a country house. In today's global village, you may be sitting there, as I was recently, with an Indian family, a Turkish pianist and Asian students. Conversations can start easily, as everybody is sharing the pepper and salt (*Sel Gris de L'Atlantique*), olive oil, jam (*confiture*), or Belgian white chocolate spread from the center of the table. On Twitter, customers can share their experiences.

In fact, the entire store has the look and feel of a country house where a family congregates alone or with friends to enjoy a continental breakfast or a simple meal. To get customers to feel at home and savor this experience, the wood tables look rough and untreated, without paint or lacquer. Walls have a warm yellow patina. The menu is handwritten on a chalkboard, as in a French bistro. The chain uses its own cabinet maker, who supplies cabinets for all stores worldwide. In the cabinets next to the entrance, they sell—you guessed it—the pepper and *sel*, olive oil, *confiture* and chocolate spread. Over the years, Le Pain Quotidien has expanded its concept, offering not just bread and bread-related food but anything that one might associate with Belgian-French country life (hearty soups, omelets and *tartines*).

CINEPOLIS: FEELING GOOD ABOUT THE MOVIE EXPERIENCE

Most people enjoy going out to the movies and the chance to escape from work or home stress. For decades movie-going has also been a staple of dating life for people around the world.

So how does a theater owner enrich this experience, get customers to savor it and expand it for the jaded customers who can now easily watch Blu-ray movies at home on their 52-inch flatscreen TVs? Offer better movies or new technology for sound, vision and scent (think Dolby, 3-D, now 4-D)? Reduce waiting lines by making it easier to buy tickets (e.g., online)? All great ideas, but real innovation calls for a total rethink of the moviegoing experience.

Consider Cinépolis, with more than 2,500 movie theaters the largest cinema company in Latin America and the fourth largest in the world. Started in Mexico and later with screens in India and Central and South America, it's now expanding to California. This luxury movie-watching experience attracted some 116.9 million visitors in 2010.

"Our goal is to delight customers, or what we call 'to be popcorn,' that is, funny, pioneering and creative," Enrique Ramírez Villalón, chairman of the board, told me, as he gave me a ride to the airport in Ixtapa after a speaking engagement with the company.

The concept is to have super-plush reclining seats with waiter/waitress service during your movie. Most people have never had this type of high-end movie experience.

It starts by purchasing tickets online or at the box office and pre-selecting seats, so there's no last-minute rush or angst over getting good seats. The comfortable meeting lounge is great for hooking up with friends for food or a drink before or after the movie. The theaters are more intimate than conventional movie houses and feature large reclining seats with footrests, giving the feeling you're in someone's living room.

But the best is yet to come, with full restaurant and bar service in the theater. Of course you can get traditional favorites like popcorn and soft drinks. But the menu expands to include specialty coffee drinks, milkshakes, gourmet finger foods, sushi, wraps, desserts, wine, spirits and beer.

"Giving the customer a 'star service' is one of the differentiators separating us from the competition and, therefore one of the key reasons that our customers prefer us," CEO Alejandro Ramírez Magaña wrote to me. "In our luxury cinema brand, Cinépolis VIP, customers enjoy the cinema because of the unforgettable moments and emotions that it provides. Our clients come to the movies and experience comfort, warmth, satisfaction of all the senses; they get good food and drinks and therefore experience the film differently."

The cost for such an experience can easily be double or triple that of a normal movie ticket. But it's an interesting way of enriching and expanding the movie-going experience in a way that high-end customers will appreciate and savor, while meeting their needs.

DIVERCITY: PLEASURE AT PLAY

Combining pleasure with play is not only for guests of W Hotels. For children, pleasure and play are most intricately connected. For young children in particular, pleasure results mostly from play. The joy that children experience when playing is obvious on the face of any child at any playground or theme park.

Divercity is a theme park for children located in Bogota, the capital of Colombia. The theme park is educational: children can act out various roles found in adult life and thus learn about their future lives. They can be bank clerks, doctors in a hospital, camera men in a television studio and, of course, firemen. They thus learn life lessons in a playful and pleasurable way.

"The children learn how to take care of their lives. They learn about money, work and being consumers," Juan Manuel Borda de Francisco, the general manager told me when he led me through the theme park.

When children arrive, they get money in the form of a check, which they can deposit in a bank account. Or they can go shopping—and when they run out of money, which happens fast, they can earn money by performing some of the jobs mentioned above. Divercity is sponsored in part by Colombian for-profit companies in the banking, retail and media sectors as well as by nonprofit organizations. They count on the fact that the pleasure experienced at this early age will eventually transfer to their brands—the beginning of a lasting consumer-brand relationship.

Also, while the kids are having fun, their parents can play on their own. Divercity has an adult waiting area where parents can engage in pleasurable activities like massages and beauty services.

CONCLUSION

A little pleasure happiness here and there as part of our daily lives can go a long way. The "Feel Good" method creates little pleasurable moments that can be the starting point of a longer and deeper relationship with customers. It does so by enriching the experience for customers, getting them to savor it and then appropriately expanding the experience.

Of course, a company that is serious about customer happiness can also dig deeper and connect with its customers more intimately. This can be done by appealing to the personal values of its customers, which we will explore in our next chapter.

4
THE "VALUES-AND-MEANING" METHOD

Connecting a company, brand or product to values can lead to a deeper, lasting sense of happiness rather than a fleeting feeling that needs to be repeated. Some companies have been very successful in appealing to the values and deep concerns of their customers—from concern for the environment to the desire to simplify their lives to discovering their spiritual selves.

THE GLOBAL YOGA CRAZE:
BREATHE IN...BREATHE OUT

For decades yoga was on the fringes of our collective social consciousness as something that only hippies or swamis did. Now an estimated 16 million Americans practice yoga.

How did yoga become the quintessential spiritual product of the West? Why are even Indians doing it again, given that until recently, many had put aside their homegrown practice? What happened in the past ten years to spark this?

I am sure true yogis have their own answers. Perhaps it has something to do with the spiritual or planetary forces at work around the turn of the new millennium. Aside from that, it seems to me that many in the post-1980s "me generation" in the US were searching for deeper meaning in their lives. Some seem to have found their spiritual grounding in yoga. Having made lots of money in the stock market and the Internet bubble (and perhaps losing just as much), they looked for value and for more meaning in their lives, other than mammon. Simultaneously, in many other countries, incomes were rising along with an emerging middle class. But as discussed in chapter 1, wealth and higher incomes do not necessarily make people happier. In fact, higher incomes spent on more products and services may set some on a hedonic treadmill. As a result, they may feel that spiritual pursuits are a better path to happiness.

Yoga became a perfect outlet: non-competitive, very grounding and seemingly non-commercial. Combine these characteristics with clever marketing and the fact that high-profile celebrities like Madonna and Sting were giving it a high media profile . . . and a very successful yoga industry was hatched.

The styles of yoga (everything from hot to not, old to new), the colorful mats and specially designed "slipless" towels, the clingy-stretchy clothing by brands such as lululemon and the upscale studios all lure the serious and the wannabes alike toward the quest for the perfect spiritual insight, balance and tranquility.[1]

Yogaworks in California is a mega-chain that's been around since 1987.[2] The very first benefit of yoga listed on their website is a "happier mood." With over 20 posh studios in the Sunshine

State and in New York, it offers more than 40 types of spiritual classes for all levels, including yoga (don't worry if you don't know Bikram from Kundalini) as well as Pilates and meditation. Whether you're young, old, single, straight, gay, married, female, male, a student or an expectant mum with a newborn or with older kids—the offerings are mind-bending. Of course, they have a shop with USD 50 mats and USD 40 dollar togs and USD 10 spray bottles of mat disinfectant with aromatic essential oils. There's a page full of YouTube testimonials explaining why clients love the place so much.

The testimonials from Earth Power Yoga are even more revealing of the marketing that goes into these studios: actresses like Renee Zellweger, Penélope Cruz and singer Jewel gush on the homepage about how they like the studio because the teacher is "really great" or simply "the best."[3]

The general effect of celebrity endorsement of yoga cannot be overestimated. High-profile people have been key drivers in the yoga industry, just as in the case of the Prius car. But the practice has also clearly caught on with ordinary customers who say the classes and the experience exceeded their expectations in healing injuries, providing a calm, contemplative environment and increasing their level of physical fitness.

When *Travel + Leisure* magazine did a story on the "25 Top Yoga Studios around the World," it was enlightening to see the offerings.[4] From Philadelphia to Phnom Penh, Cape Town to Copenhagen—they were all slick, upscale establishments. Many had rewards programs, retail shops (for the latest gear, books, bags or DVDs), and cafés or juice bars.

Airyoga in Zurich and Munich offers workshops and retreats.[5] London's triyoga advertises "yoga holidays."[6] Nearly all offer some sort of spa treatments or bodywork. This is more than a mere hobby or a way to get in touch with inner feelings; it's a lifestyle phenomenon where unhappy customers walk in and happy, balanced ones walk out.

The cradle of modern yoga is the Yoga Institute in Mumbai, India.[7] Founded in 1918 by Shri Yogendraji, it claims to be the oldest organized center of yoga in the world. Here, surprisingly, yoga has not reached the fever pitch in terms of marketing and snazziness that it has in most places in the West. The Yoga Institute merely hums along, teaching very dedicated and earnest people their asanas. Another yoga studio, Sivananda Yoga Vedanta Nataraja Centre, which has five centers across India, is also decidedly low-key by modern, Western standards.[8] The website is complete but has the look of being self-designed. It has a boutique and a library, and offers yoga vacations, similar to what's offered elsewhere, although the emphasis appears to be more on the yoga itself than on appearances and products. For example, the centers are located in old houses, not flashy newly purpose-built studios. Customers go there seeking an authentic experience. Perhaps this is the next stage of yoga happiness: back to the basics and utmost simplicity.

Breathe in . . . breathe out. . . .

BACK TO ARISTOTLE

As discussed earlier, happiness was of extreme importance to the Greeks. Aristotle viewed happiness as "the meaning and the purpose of life, the whole aim and end of human existence." He also tied happiness closely to virtue. Happiness was seen as the outcome of a consciously lived life, characterized by the five cardinal virtues of courage, piety, temperance, wisdom and justice. Happiness was about *eudaimonia,* not hedonism.

Aristotle was not alone. The eudaemonistic view of happiness was also stressed by subsequent philosophers and spiritual leaders. "Happiness is when what you think, what you say, and what you do are in harmony," Mahatma Gandhi wrote. And the Dalai Lama said, "I see happiness mainly in the sense of deep satisfaction." The eudaemonistic view of happiness in positive psychology is also closely tied to personal values and meaning. If an individual can realize his or her fullest human potential, he can thus find what Victor Frankl has called "the ultimate values."[9]

THE NATURE OF VALUES

What exactly do we mean by "values"? Professor Shalom Schwartz, one of the most prominent psychologists studying values, defines them as "desirable trans-situational goals, varying in importance, that serve as guiding principles in the life of a person or another social entity."[10] Values are thus broad goals that people try to achieve. Yet they vary in importance among individuals; your core values may not be mine.

Schwartz also engaged in the challenging task of identifying which values are recognized in cultures around the world. To accomplish this, he first examined the work of another prominent psychologist, Milton Rokeach, who had distinguished various so-called terminal values (e.g., harmony, equality, family, concern for the environment). Schwartz also conducted questionnaire studies in different cultures and looked at religious and philosophical writings. He ultimately found ten cross-culturally important values. Researchers in more than 30 countries have already used his system to study the relationship between values and all sorts of behaviors such as use of alcohol, condoms and drugs; moral, religious and sexual behavior; choice of university majors, occupation and medical specialty; and participation in sports, social contacts and voting.

Here are the ten values (and associated goals):

1. **Self-Direction**

   Independent thought and action; choosing, creating, exploring.

2. **Stimulation**

   Excitement, novelty and challenge in life.

3. **Hedonism**

   Pleasure and sensuous gratification of oneself.

4. **Achievement**

   Personal success through demonstrating competence according to social standards.

5. **Power**

   Social status and prestige, control or dominance over people and resources.

6. **Security**

   Safety, harmony and stability of society, of relationships and of self.

7. **Conformity**

   Restraint of actions, inclinations and impulses likely to upset or harm others and violate social expectations or norms.

8. **Tradition**

   Respect, commitment and acceptance of the customs and ideas that traditional culture or religion provide.

9. **Benevolence**

   Preserving and enhancing the welfare of those
   with whom one is in frequent personal contact (the
   "in-group").

10. **Universalism**

   Understanding, appreciation, tolerance and protection for
   the welfare of all people and for nature.

These broad values lead to specific actions. If self-direction is important to you, you may set up your own business. If achievement is one of your core values, you work hard. If benevolence is one of your values, you engage in social activities that benefit others.

Moreover, values are not cold, rational beliefs; they are closely tied to emotions. Self-direction or achievement or power can make us proud; stimulation or hedonism can make us feel excited; security, conformity and tradition can make us feel comfortable. Benevolence and universalism can make us feel empathetic. In turn, values can make us happy because products and services associated with values trigger positive feelings.

Interestingly, values are also partly related to personality. Schwartz and his colleagues examined relationships between the Big Five human personality traits (openness, conscientiousness, extroversion, agreeableness and emotional stability) and values. They found that agreeableness correlates positively with benevolence and traditional values. Openness correlates with self-direction and universalism, extroversion with achievement and stimulation, and conscientiousness with achievement and conformity.[11]

Finally, note that hedonism (the focus of chapter 3) is also one of Schwartz's ten values, with pleasure and sensuous gratification as associated goals. Hedonism can thus be one's guiding principle in life. If it is one of your values, you may not end up on the regrettable hedonic treadmill. Rather, hedonism is, in an existential sense, your raison d'être and may make you permanently happy.

As Schwartz wrote, values can also serve as guiding principles of a social entity—for example, a company. Let's look at how values that are incorporated into a company's culture can become a point of competitive differentiation and customer trust.

WEGELIN & CO.: COMBINING
TRADITIONAL AND MODERN VALUES[12]

Wegelin & Co. is Switzerland's oldest bank, located in the city of St. Gallen. It was founded in 1741 and is a key player in Switzerland's private banking industry. Wegelin specializes in wealth management for private individuals and asset management for pension funds.

As one enters Wegelin & Co.'s headquarters, as I did when I wrote a case study about the company a couple of years ago, one instantly feels the bank's long history and traditional values. The heavy door opens slowly, revealing an austere entrance hall. The wooden floors creak. Historic paintings hang on the walls. Bank clerks whisper. Above the two cashier counters, ornately carved griffins stand as silent guardians of history—everything you might expect from a bank with such a pedigree.

What you might not expect is that the bank is also, to use Schwartz's terminology, quite "self-directed" and innovative. Wegelin has state-of-the-art IT infrastructure, including software with open-system architecture and a graphical interface.

Most important is the core value of using a client-centered approach to manage customer relationships. Following Schwartz's scheme, we may call this "financial benevolence." Dr. Konrad Hummler, the longest-serving of Wegelin's current managing partners, is personally responsible for the bank's assets and believes in maintaining a close relationship with clients. He rejects the client-segmentation schemes practiced by larger banks. When I spoke with him, Hummler was adamant about his views on client relations and segmentation:

> *"Consider what segmentation in private banking really means: You don't treat your customers equally. You give more and better service to some of your customers. Segmentation disrupts client relationships with unpredictable ripple effects."*

As a result, client relationships at Wegelin are based on continuity, trust and dialogue. In the midst of the global financial maelstrom in the late 2000s, Wegelin, unlike UBS and Credit Suisse, steered a steady course, staying away from risky financial instruments. Another aspect of straight talk that instills trust. Since joining the bank in 1991, Hummler has authored the periodic *Wegelin Investment Commentaries*. The *Commentaries* reflect Hummler's personal style and he wants them to be educational, informative and honest. Then, there is the dialogue with and among customers, which happens over bratwurst and beer rather than caviar and champagne. Most importantly, relationships at Wegelin are personal. They decided not to launch an online trading platform, feeling that the client base of mostly 50- to 60-year-old customers would not use such a system.

Instead they focused on developing an online information system through which clients would be able to access current research and various portfolio and risk reports. Finally, even when tempted—for example, in the expansion phase of the industry in the 2000s—Wegelin focused exclusively on domestic customers and did not expand its services and geographical reach. Wegelin's value-driven approach provides consistency and ongoing rewarding relationships with customers.

CONSUMER VALUES AND TRENDS

The general values identified in all cultures by Schwartz are important, though not all of them can be easily tied to the purchase and consumption of products and services. There are other, more specific values that are of particular relevance in the context of buying and consumption. Here are three values that are currently quite important to customers: first, the value of preserving the environment, being green and reducing the carbon footprint; second, simplicity; and, finally, the most important value for many consumers, the value of "value."

Consider each value trend through a practical example of a company that has capitalized on it.

BRITA: THE CASE FOR CLEANER AND "GREENER" WATER
In the water category, a mind-boggling value shift from "lifestyle" to "concern for the environment" has occurred in just ten years.

In the late 1990s, everyone was concerned about having the right kind of bottled water in hand. There were many competing brands, and it seemed that everyone was jumping into the lifestyle water market. Back then, my MBA students were showing up to class with all sorts of different water bottles.

That was the heyday of Poland Spring, Crystal Geyser and Fiji, and more obscure brands like Spa, Appalachian and Equator. I featured this lifestyle trend and these brands in my 1999 book *Experiential Marketing.*

However, all of these products had an immense, and by then well-documented, carbon footprint. As US consumers finally jumped on the "green" bandwagon in the mid-2000s, they asked, "Why do I need to buy this?" This new trend, focused on the environment as a new value to consumers, sent the bottled-water industry running for cover. Some manufacturers, like Poland Spring, have since tried to improve their environmental record with new bottle design (30 percent less carbon footprint and so on).

But the bottled water industry remains a resource-intensive business that, as you may know, is an energy gobbler. The entire chain, from manufacturing the bottles to putting the water into them to getting the product into stores, is eco-unfriendly. Some 1.5 million barrels of crude oil are used to make polyethylene terephthalate (PET) water bottles around the world each year, fuelling an industry in which roughly USD 35 billion is spent buying the stuff in developed countries alone.[13]

According to analysis done by the Pacific Institute, it takes two thousand times more energy to produce a bottle of water than it does to produce tap water.[14] Many people intend to recycle disposable water bottles; however, 69 percent of bottled water containers still end up in the trash.[15]

Since it takes so much plastic, and about two liters of water, to make one liter of bottled water, environmentalists have decried the industry as wasteful and as largely unnecessary in most developed countries. Of course, in certain parts of the world (whether because of underdeveloped infrastructure or natural disasters), clean drinking water is a serious problem, and bottled water can be a realistic solution. But in many first world countries, tap water is tested regularly by municipal governments, is absolutely fine to drink and does not cost a penny. This leaves it to eco-conscious H_2O drinkers to consider their choices. In places where water is already purified, sometimes all that's needed is simple filtration to take out a bit of smell or bad taste.

Enter Brita. The company is the world's market leader in portable household water filtration. Since 1966 they've made water pitchers, kettles and tap attachments. Originally founded in Germany, the ubiquitous filter pitchers are now in every corner of the globe. Their products are not meant to purify extremely bad or even questionable water. Rather, they say their mission is "optimizing tap water."[16]

So, like many urbanites, I have a Brita filled in my refrigerator, ready for action when the taste of my tap water needs a little help. And many of my students these days don't show up to class with disposable plastic water bottles just purchased from the convenience store. They bring reusable, recycled bottles or Nalgene bottles filled at the water fountain across the hall or from their Brita pitchers at home. They've learned that tap water is just fine, with a little help.

As one of Brita's taglines says: "The Better Water Tastes, the More You're Bound to Drink."[17] This idea makes their customers very happy: they're using a product that is directly helping them avoid having to purchase disposable polyethylene terephthalate (PET) bottles. The company says that one Brita pitcher filter can replace as many as 300 standard 16.9-ounce bottles; the average Brita pitcher filters about 240 gallons of water each year, saving about 1,800 disposable water bottles.[18] Thus, Brita customers feel good about themselves for having made a positive contribution to the environment, society and the planet.

An opportunistic advertising campaign, the "Filter for Good" 2008 campaign, reinforced Brita's approach. It reported how much oil was used to make plastic water bottles, graphically showing women and men with oil oozing from their mouths. The company said that some 281,000,000 PET bottles have been spared as a result of people going to their www.filterforgood.com website and taking a pledge not to use disposable bottles.[19]

In addition to helping customers feel good about using their products, Brita also gives back to their local and international communities, which engenders more customer goodwill. In 2007, Brita agreed to support a UNICEF (United Nations International Children's Emergency Fund) project to provide and enhance drinking water in rural Vietnamese villages. The project targeted clean drinking water for at least 60,000 children. In 2010, Brita worked with fashion designer Orla Kiely to support the Breast Cancer Care Charity. The partnership resulted in a limited-edition hydration pack containing a water filter jug, three filter cartridges and a reusable water bottle designed by Kiely and made of 100 percent recycled materials. For every pack sold, Brita donated GBP 1 to the charity. They also partner with the Surfrider Foundation, the organization that works to keep North American waterways clean. Brita and bottle maker Nalgene have donated USD 200,000 to Surfrider to help clean streams, rivers, lakes and oceans.

All of these efforts have made their environmentally conscious customers happy about using the product, as well as supporting the company's efforts to change the way people think about and use drinking water.

But the company has not been controversy-free. The ad campaign in 2008 described earlier provoked strong opinions, leading some critics to complain that the Brita products do not filter out every possible contaminant and that the company misleads consumers into believing that tap water is safe. Proponents, however, say that any effort to get people away from using disposable plastic bottles is worth it.

PHILIPS: SENSE AND SIMPLICITY

Another consumer value trend is simplicity. Many people feel overwhelmed by the complexity of modern life—both in their professional and private lives. They want to simplify. Consumers may even feel overwhelmed by too much product choice. My colleague at Columbia Business School, management professor Sheena Iyengar, claims in her research, and in her book titled *The Art of Choosing*, that consumers are happier with fewer rather than more choices.[20]

The simplicity trend has even reached large organizations with multiple product lines. They are trying to communicate a simplicity brand promise to their customers.

For example, Philips, the Netherlands-based company, has a broad product line for B2B and B2C, ranging from light bulbs and lighting equipment to electric toothbrushes and shavers to medical equipment such as devices for anesthesiology, cardiology or surgery. Many of its products are for daily commercial or private use. Because they are well designed and innovative, these products are likely to make some business customers happy—

especially with the company's award-winning lighting systems for retail customers.

Yet Philips felt that it lacked a consistent way of delivering an integrated Philips brand experience to its customers. Now, they finally feel like they have found it and have expressed it in a new corporate vision: "Simply making a difference to people's lives."[21]

Except for the "simply," it's similar to their old ad slogan, "We make things better," and reminds me of what is arguably the most successful corporate ad campaign of all time, US competitor GE's "We bring good things to life."

So, how significant is "simply"? It depends on how you look at it. As a communication campaign, it may have sharpened the Philips image. Not bad, but limited. But if viewed as a chance to unite the company around a theme valued by customers and even adding value as an idea within Philips, then I feel it is a winning proposition. Think of it: simplicity as a corporate value calls for the design of simple, appealing and intuitive products; customers can sense their use instantly. Hence the brand slogan: "Sense and Simplicity." Moreover, it also calls for simplifying service, product lines, corporate bureaucracies, meetings and the like, especially in B2B settings. If taken seriously, a "simple" word can create magic in an organization.

UNIQLO: UNIQUE + VALUE

Finally, there is the classic consumer value called "value"—that is, a good price/quality relation. This value is not really new, but it's always in fashion. Consumers are always looking for a good deal—whether shopping at the low end or the high end. Assuming other criteria are met (product features, quality, technology, image, brand appeal), receiving value is important to consumers.

But here's a new twist: getting both uniqueness and value in the same product. Many stores try to claim this territory, and a handful succeeds. It used to be that you could just offer a low price and be successful in, for example, casual fashion retailing. Nowadays, the motto is to shop cheap, but with style. UNIQLO (meaning "unique" and "low") stands out in that respect. The homegrown Japanese company is well known in Asian capital cities as well as in London, Paris, Moscow, New York and Chicago. In the late 1990s, the brand and strategy were modeled after the GAP, and when I met with top management then, the company was in trouble. The company had overexpanded and was closing stores. Since then, they have entirely revamped their strategy, embarked on an aggressive international expansion campaign outside Japan, and are now competing on a global scale with European casual-wear retailers such as H&M, Zara and Mango.

UNIQLO's founder, Tadashi Yanai, has said he wants to empower people by allowing them to create a unique style. What attracts customers to the brand is the combination of hot fashion and low prices. UNIQLO owns the entire operation, from sourcing raw materials to the design center to manufacturing and retail outlets. They say that controlling the supply chain in this way allows them to react quickly to changes in the market and gives their customers timely, well-priced products.

For example, consider their UT project.[22] The idea is to "bring today's culture to the world." The UT Project was launched in 2007 in Harajuku, Tokyo's edgy youth-culture district, with the opening of an avant-garde convenience store for T-shirts. In parallel, UNIQLO started to feature limited-edition T-shirts in its flagship stores, for example, in Ginza, Tokyo's main shopping district. Nowadays, one thousand styles are introduced each year; these T-shirts are available from Osaka to Shanghai to Paris to New York City. They are unique and inexpensive T-shirts (UTs) featuring all sorts of categories: art, music, photography, design, manga characters and iconic brands (e.g., shirts with global brand logos). Their T-shirts bring today's culture to the world.

Making customers happy is Uniqlo's declared goal. When they opened a new flagship store on Regent Street in London in 2011, the slogan "Uniqlo makes Regent Street happy" was blasted on all communications. During the opening day of the store, customers could get a complimentary "Happy Breakfast," and a "Happy Machine" released products at rock-bottom prices every few hours. The brochure designed for the opening events stated, "Uniqlo is clothes that suit your values."

THE THREE STEPS OF THE
"VALUES-AND-MEANING" METHOD

The "Values-and-Meaning" method is a general process for connecting companies, brands and products to people's values to create meaning happiness. The first step identifies relevant personal values and then gets customers to focus on these values, which are issues of deeper concern to them. It can also contextualize the offer by placing it in a broader social context.

The method thus includes three steps: (1) identifying relevant values, (2) value focusing and (3) contextualizing.

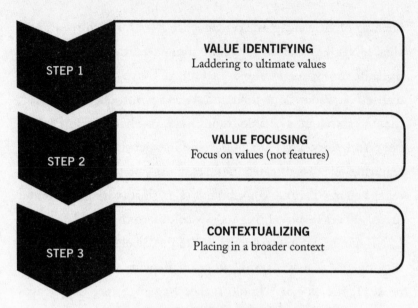

**FIGURE 4. THREE STEPS OF THE
"VALUES-AND-MEANING" METHOD**

STEP 1: IDENTIFYING RELEVANT VALUES

Identifying customer values is the first step in any marketing approach focused on customer values. This can be accomplished by using the "laddering" technique. Laddering was first introduced by clinical psychologists in the 1960s as a method of understanding people's core values and beliefs. Marketing researchers then adapted the laddering method for use in consumer research. They constructed a means-end chain with a series of "why" questions, ranging from attributes to consumption benefits (or consequences) to personal values.

For example, a consumer may be asked why they like an iPhone, or why they prefer an iPhone to another smartphone. The consumer may say, "Because it has lots of apps." Apps are product attributes. But why does the consumer like to have lots of them?

Perhaps because they are fun—which is a benefit or consequence. And why is fun important? Because it adds a sense of excitement and novelty to life. Now we have established that, for this consumer, stimulation may be the ultimate value-purchase driver.

For another customer, it may be power (control and dominance by having apps and information at their fingertips) or conformity (following the norms of a reference group). Knowing what matters to which customer will help you to position the product, choose communications and social media, and design the user interface accordingly—that is, in a stimulating, playful way, a powerful way or in a way that seems to be the style of the reference group.

It is important to understand consumers' personal values and how they vary among segments. Early on, the core customer segment of BlackBerry was the business and enterprise segment; they understood that segment's values very well. The achievement-oriented business customer liked the BlackBerry because of its basic functionality, such as a keyboard for typing e-mail messages, an efficient calendar for making appointments, and easy integration with Microsoft Outlook.

As the market for smartphones grew, ordinary consumers with different values entered the market. Then came PDAs (personal digital assistants), and BlackBerry failed to understand the new, emerging values. While the market was still growing, BlackBerry was gradually losing market share. BlackBerry's market share peaked in the third quarter of 2009 (21 percent), but two years later, it was down to 14 percent.

BlackBerry even began to neglect its core customer segment. New software on the Bold model came with bugs and unnecessarily complex features. The company lost track of what had originally made its customers happy. A once highly loyal customer base was abandoning the brand. After a series of outages, industry analysts declared it a "broken brand." Over the years, other consumer electronics companies, including Nokia, Motorola and Sony, have run into similar issues and lost some of their once-happy customers.[23]

STEP 2: VALUE FOCUSING

Once you've identified the personal values that matter to your customers, you are ready to move on to the second step of the "Values-and-Meaning" method: value focusing.

This is a technique to direct customers' attention away from product features and focus on their personal values. Value focusing directs customers to the values that they personally appreciate in a way that enhances positive feelings while avoiding negative feelings or cultural taboos. Remember the Prudential case discussed in chapter 2? They steered clear of one of the negative feelings associated with life insurance—death.

Earlier, we discussed the "green" trend in the water category that resulted in consumers drinking less bottled water. The trend occurred because consumers shifted focus to new values that were important to them. Reports and studies drew their attention to the fact that many of the bottled waters were not always as pure as the proverbial artesian spring, and as advertisers would have them believe. Moreover, a well-publicized four-year study of bottled water in the US, done by the Natural Resources Defense Council, found that one-fifth of the 103 water products tested contained synthetic organic chemicals such as the neurotoxin xylene and the possible carcinogen and neurotoxin styrene.[24] Moreover, word spread on the Internet that much of today's bottled water comes from a city tap anyway, not from some distant, scenic natural aquifer or babbling brook. These findings, and the fact that bottled waters have a massive carbon footprint and can be more expensive per gallon than gasoline, all led consumers to alternative drinking-water sources.[25]

STEP 3: CONTEXTUALIZING

In addition to identifying core values and getting the customer to focus on his or her values, you must contextualize your offer for the customer.

Step 3 of the "Values-and-Meaning" method, contextualizing, means placing your product or service in a broader context and showing the customer that you are truly sensitive to their value and the causes they care about, and not just focused on getting money out of their pockets.

In contextualizing, you need to think big. Consider IBM. It may still be called "International Business Machines Corp.," a provider of information technology products and services. But the company views itself as providing solutions for a smarter planet.

A "smarter planet" means, as IBM chairman, CEO and president Sam Palmisano explained during a 2010 speech in London, that "intelligence is being infused into the systems and processes that enable services to be delivered; physical goods to be developed, manufactured, bought and sold; everything from people and money to oil, water and electrons, intersecting where billions of people work and live." In other words, the computational power of large computers interconnected on the Internet to small and inexpensive digital devices produces massive data clumps that can be turned into intelligence that raises the quality of products, companies and cities.

In 2009, IBM's Smarter Planet initiative created 1,200 examples of smarter solutions. They helped to deliver transport congestion solutions; smarter healthcare systems; and more risk control, efficiency and better customer service in financial institutions while reducing retailers' supply-chain costs.

IBM revamped its website into a rich-content site presenting information on the Smarter Planet initiative. It has organized hundreds of Smarter Planet conferences for CEOs, CIOs and civic leaders.[26] The Smarter Planet Blog shows bottom-line results by presenting proof points and data.

As Palmisano explained,

"Building a smarter planet is realistic precisely because it is so refreshingly non-ideological. Yes, debates will continue to rage on many contentious issues in our society—from energy, to security, to climate change, to healthcare, to the economy. Yes, we will surely continue to deliberate, for some time to come, over the role of government, of the private sector, of the new constituencies emerging across civil society. There are serious and worthy perspectives on all sides of these controversies. But no matter which viewpoint one shares—or which ultimately prevails in any given society or industry—the system that results will need to be smarter—more transparent, more efficient, more accessible, more equitable, more resilient. And that's one final reason for hope: making our planet smarter is in everyone's interest."

THE RISK OF DIVIDING VALUES

Because values are closely tied to emotions, values can divide people, and therefore may be tricky to manage. For example, while Whole Foods Market (WFM) is generally well supported by its customers (as discussed in chapter 1), sometimes the company reaches out in ways that attract criticism. In a bid to engage their diverse communities, WFM ran this web post:

> *"Check out this great recount of the San Francisco Gay Pride Parade. Many of the Team Members from our stores in the Bay Area participated . . . and it sounds (and looks) like they had a BLAST!"*

This was generally a hit with the WFM community, but it also registered negative reaction from the 400 respondents:

> *"WF . . . did you intend to alienate and lose your conservative customers by posting this?"*

> *"So Whole Foods is in the business of promoting natural food and unnatural sex . . . good going, Whole Foods!"*

To which WFM replied:

> *"We appreciate all the feedback. While we do celebrate all walks of life and diversity at Whole Foods Market, we are sorry if our post offended you."*

But no issue has ignited more controversy for WFM than its recent stand with the US Food and Drug Administration to "coexist" with genetic engineering of food and genetically modified organisms (GMOs), where seeds are modified in the laboratory to enhance production.

The organic food movement has opposed this for many years, citing human and environmental reasons. And this very movement is the cornerstone of WFM's retail success. Now detractors feel that the company is turning its back on the cause, as well as not labeling all of its food correctly. Critics say 25 percent of WFM sales of their so-called natural products may contain GMOs, but are not labeled as such.

Not surprisingly, the company sees it differently and posted a long letter in response to the many critical media articles. It read, in part: "We supported a path of coexistence, not because it's a perfect path, but because it's the only viable path that would ensure our ongoing ability to provide non-GMO foods."[27]

This prompted nearly all negative replies on Facebook, many of which were quite emotional.

"It makes me so sad . . ."

"I will no longer purchase any products from Whole Foods and the other companies that caved in to big money. You were one of my favorite retailers but now you are just like all the others. I will search harder for providers that resist perks and money from polluters such as Monsanto."

"I am saddened that this happened and that you 'fell a little' just to have your way & say, thinking the Gov. would go your way partly, when they rarely do!!"

"DO NOT BUY FROM WHOLE FOODS MARKET!!!!!!!"

The jury is still out on whether this issue will have a long-lasting impact on the happiness and loyalty of WFM shoppers. But it will be an interesting case study on the limits of customer loyalty when values are involved.

WFM is not the only company that faces scrutiny. Amazon. com promotes and defends the value of free information and distribution, but in 2010, somebody wanted to sell *The Pedophile's Guide to Love and Pleasure* on its site. What should Amazon do? Or, to take a purely hypothetical example, what if you are the Blue Moon Smoothies company and you harvest a rare antioxidant ingredient for your smoothies that is available only in the high mountains of Shakmakistan, and now a military junta has taken over the country and an activist group calls for a boycott? It is not easy to get it right when you are dealing with values. Values can divide. By the way, after some delay, Amazon pulled the controversial book from its site.

CONCLUSION

Connecting companies, brands and products to customer values and concerns offers businesses an opportunity to relate to customers more deeply and permanently. Because values are emotional, motivational and closely tied to a person's identity, it is unlikely that customers will forget about them. However, people will change and grow, and new generations will come along with new ideas. That's how new value trends will arise. The "Values-and-Meaning" method can help you identify relevant values, get customers to focus on them and contextualize your offer for the customer.

A key challenge for any business is to make sure that customers remain actively engaged with the company and feel happy when they are engaged. I will address this challenge in the next chapter.

5

THE "ENGAGEMENT" METHOD

Customer engagement has become a "hot" concept in business and marketing. The term was originally popularized by fast-moving consumer goods (FMCG) companies and their ad agencies. When they realized that mass communications were losing their relative impact, they were forced to redirect their marketing toward direct customer contacts to drive purchase and consumption.

THE "OPEN HAPPINESS" CAMPAIGN

On January 21, 2009, the Coca-Cola Company launched its "Open Happiness" campaign with this exuberant press release:

> *"The Coca-Cola Company today invites the billions of people around the world who love to pause and refresh themselves with a Coke to 'Open Happiness' and continue to enjoy one of life's simple pleasures. That is the central message for 'Open Happiness'—Coca-Cola's new*

global integrated marketing campaign that launches in the U.S. this week."

The "Open Happiness" campaign goes far beyond simple communication marketing seeking to spread a happiness message. To be sure, the campaign has a communication aspect: it aims to make Coke consumers feel good and add as much meaning to life as there can be for a soft drink by linking pleasure to the benefit of refreshment. But it's also about making Coca-Cola a relevant part of people's daily lives by activating consumers, immersing them in the Coca-Cola experience and allowing them to share this experience with friends and strangers alike.

Consider the following elements of the "Open Happiness" campaign. In one example, a Coke machine is installed at a university cafeteria. As students insert their coins to buy a bottle of Coke, wonderful and magical things happen: some receive six or more bottles for the price of one, a real human hand dispenses flowers to a young coed, a hot take-away pizza with Cokes is dispensed to another unsuspecting person; a box of popcorn, a Twister game, a six-foot Italian submarine sandwich—all dispensed through the large vending slot (Cokes, too, of course). Every recipient is awestruck by the unexpected windfall; some even give the vending machine a hug. Each time they share the excess with the other people in the cafeteria, it creates communal happiness and buzz. Everyone has huge smiles. The immediate effect is an off-line experience with everyone around benefiting from the "Happiness Machine."

To be sure, the campaign is not just about making a few students in a cafeteria happy. The company is relying on the viral spreading of their generosity. By December 2011 over 4 million people had watched the YouTube video of this happening at a US university, while 850,000 watched the version that was taped at a London university.[1] Each time there's a tagline proclaiming, "Where will the happiness strike next?" You never know when one of their dispensing machines will be extra-generous, so perhaps you should try all of them!

"The purpose of the campaign is to engage consumers in their daily lives," Shay Drohan, Senior VP of Global Sparkling Brands, told me when I spoke with him. "With this new campaign, we want consumers to have a Coke, chill out for a moment, and be a little happier than a couple of minutes ago."

Another clever manifestation of this campaign was the 2x1 "Friendship Machines."[2] Freakishly tall Coke vending machines were put in key locations across seven countries with a clear message that if you bought one drink, the second would be free. The challenge was that the coin slot was so far out of reach that everyone needed help to insert the coins. Without help, there would be no Coke. All of a sudden, people were engaging each other and working together to get a Coke. Brilliant, when you consider that the typical two-for-one sale in a grocery store aisle is hardly engaging and does very little to create any connection between the brand and the consumer (beyond "it's cheap, so I'll buy it").

When the "Friendship Machines" hit, there was not a sourpuss in sight, as friends and strangers hoisted one another on shoulders to activate the machine, bonding with Coke in the process. They activated both interpersonal relationships and the customers' connection with the brand. The company says that 800 Cokes were dispersed at each machine within nine hours (1,075 percent more than at the ordinary Coke machine). The campaign also turned this brand activation into online content; thousands of comments were posted on blogs and social networking sites around the world, and the videos got some 700,000 YouTube hits.

In another instance, a big, red Coca-Cola "Happiness Truck" with only a large "push" button and vending door on the back drove to various working-class neighborhoods in Brazil and the Philippines. [3] At each stop, it dispensed everything from cold Cokes to soccer balls, beach toys and even a full-size surfboard, depending on the neighborhood. Again, the people who witnessed this were all smiles and shared their experience with those around them.

Coke's "Happiness Store" had a similar outcome. [4] When someone purchased a Coke product out of the refrigerator case at a particular mini-mart, special lighting was activated, generating a spontaneous party atmosphere. Consumers were given more Cokes than they could possibly carry. This prompted them to engage with other people in the store, giving away the extra Cokes.

"Throughout its 125 years of history, Coca-Cola has always had happiness as one of its core values. This campaign builds on that heritage and provides a locally relevant expression of this happiness," Drohan said.

Interestingly, Coke Great Britain launched its latest ad campaign online first, with the hope of the campaign going viral even before the more traditional ads would be launched. [5] Coke said it was starting online to reach the key teen demographic.

Drohan told me that the company tracks the impact on a global basis. In markets where Coke is already strong, such as Mexico and Brazil, the goal is to sustain the strength of the brand. In emerging markets such as Indonesia, the campaign is supposed to strengthen the brand and make it relevant to its target segments. By all counts, the campaign continues to do very well.

The Coca-Cola Company really gets it. With its fabulously simple and creative campaign, they have distilled the essence of their brand and released it into the community. The innovative engagement components of the campaign may serve as a best-practice benchmark for happiness engagement campaigns for years to come.

WHAT IS CUSTOMER ENGAGEMENT?

Customer engagement, both in B2C and B2B markets, is associated with behavior. It implies, as pragmatist linguists might say, a "performative act." That means it's not just about saying or thinking or feeling something—it's about doing.

Customer engagement can also connote an involvement, a promise or a commitment. This involvement can be with the company, with a brand or with one another. When companies declare that they are engaging customers, they are promising something. They are making a commitment to communicate and interact directly with customers. Conversely, when customers engage with companies and their brands, they are becoming actively involved; they are committing to doing business with the company. Engagement is thus not just about a trial run, but repeat interactions, loyalty, world-of-mouth marketing and long-term active relationships.

ATTITUDES AND BEHAVIORS

Customer engagement deals with a perennial marketing and business problem: how to get from feeling and thinking to action and habitual behavior. In fact, this question has dogged behavioral researchers for years, well beyond the marketing and business communities. Numerous studies have shown that the relationship between attitudes and behavior is weak. Moreover, several meta-analyses have been conducted. Meta-analysis is a statistical integration of data that has been accumulated across many different studies. It controls for measurement and sampling errors that may distort the results of individual studies, revealing the actual relationship between the variables. Controlling for such biases, the correlation between attitudes and behaviors has, nonetheless, been weak: around 0.38 in several meta-analyses.

To put it in the context of this book, customers may be happy because they experienced pleasurable moments with you or because you gave them a product that appeals to their values, and therefore, is meaningful to them. But that does not mean that they take the next step, which is to express their happiness behaviorally and repeatedly buy what you are selling. Happiness can be a passive state; customers need to be engaged so that pleasure and meaning have lasting behavioral effects.

How can the relationship be strengthened? How can we get customers to move from thinking and feeling to actual behavior? Recently psychologists conducted a meta-analysis that did not just measure the relationship between attitudes and behavior in the aggregate, but examined different types of attitudes. The finding: the correlation could be significantly increased to 0.52. The correlations between attitudes and behavior got stronger when attitudes were "accessible" and "stable over time."

What do psychologists mean by "attitude accessibility" and "attitude stability"? Attitudes are most accessible when people have direct experience with the objects and express their attitudes frequently, and most stable when people form their attitudes based on behavior-relevant information.

These findings have important implications for how to engage consumers. First, direct experience matters and you must therefore create as many touchpoint contacts as possible with customers. Moreover, passive engagement using traditional mass communications and even new media won't work as well as live events and direct interactions. Finally, and most importantly, whenever you are in touch with customers, you must make sure that you first activate their behavior, then you immerse them in the experience and finally get them to share their experiences with other customers.

This leads us to the three steps for engaging customers, which describe the process of getting customers to become actively involved with your company and your brands.

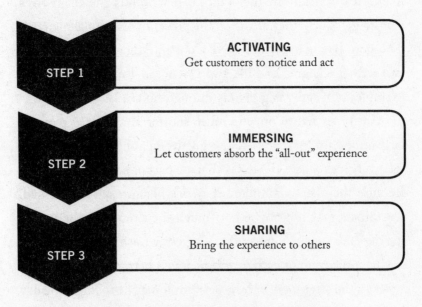

FIGURE 5. THE "ENGAGEMENT" METHOD

THE THREE STEPS OF THE
"ENGAGEMENT" METHOD

STEP 1: ACTIVATING

Customer activation gets customers to notice a product, brand or marketing campaign, and to act on it. Usually the customer who is quite familiar with the brand pays little attention to it. The brand has shifted to the background. Activating the brand means returning it to the foreground, to the customer's focus of attention, and thus increasing the chance of re-purchase.

This can be done through small tweaks in the product design (Amazon's One-Click button), in retailing through point-of-purchase displays (signs saying "Grab Me Now" in 7-Eleven stores), and of course through various online and offline communication campaigns. At times, it may also be important to remind customers of past positive experiences, even childhood or teenage memories, to reactivate the brand. When brands give themselves a nostalgic touch, they are using the power of emotional memory. The new Beetle and the MINI Cooper, Adidas and Converse, and retro-packaging of Tide and Downy in Target stores are all examples of reactivating brands through nostalgia.

Customer activation, on a much shorter time scale, is particularly important for so-called low-involvement brands, such as the relatively inexpensive FMCGs that are part of people's daily lives. Because they are so common, they risk being taken for granted. Customers may not notice how much their mood in the morning depends on applying a refreshing body wash in the shower or having a nice cup of coffee, or how much better they feel after a snack in the afternoon, or how pleasant it may be to finish the day by reading *Vogue* or *Sports Illustrated* before going to sleep. They may have always done this, and as a result, these experiences may have become habit. Of course, savoring (a technique we encountered in chapter 3) may help to re-attract the attention of some consumers to such moments. But not everybody has time to savor while getting ready in the morning, while rushing around in the afternoon or when getting tired in the evening. In this case, something more drastic is needed—perhaps changes to the form, flavor or design of the product itself.

One really drastic form of consumer activation is a brand relaunch. This can be tricky, though. While it does shake up consumers and get them to pay attention, it may risk the comfort—and positive affect—of familiarity. Coca-Cola's move to New Coke is a classic example of how it can go horribly wrong. Tropicana's disastrous packaging design change in 2009 is a more recent example.

As Stuart Elliott, the ad critic of the *New York Times*, wrote, "It took 24 years, but PepsiCo now has its own version of New Coke."[6] For that many years, PepsiCo's Tropicana brand had used the familiar orange and straw, and the brand logo with the leaf, on its packaging. In January 2009, however, they hired design guru Peter Arnett, head of Omnicom's Arnett Group, to redesign the packaging. The new design gave up valuable design equities and reduced the size of the logo. It replaced the outside of the orange with an image of squeezed juice and added a "squeeze cup" allowing the user to ergonomically experience the squeezing of an orange. To consumers, the new packaging looked like a generic or store brand, and from certain angles, it wasn't even clear that it was orange juice. After seven weeks, with sales down drastically, PepsiCo pulled the new packaging. The case significantly damaged Arnett's reputation, though he did not seem to care. He was quoted as saying, "Can you imagine such mishegoss over a freaking box of juice?"

To be sure, it is important to rejuvenate the brand at times, but as the Tropicana example shows, it may not be a good idea to entirely re-invent it. Re-inventions should be left up to brand extensions, not the core brand.

Consumer activations are also critical when a consumer has just acquired a product or brand for the first time. All of its fun and meaning may come from using it. Credit cards are a good example—or at least, that's how credit card companies want us to think about their products. As a result, they have sophisticated customer activation campaigns to get consumers to use their cards. It actually all starts with a simple process of activating the card. The initial activation is followed by specially developed marketing programs, including discount programs with particular merchants, national promotions, special offers for certain targeted segments, tie-ins with reward programs, special services, various bill-payment options and the like. All of this, just to make sure you won't forget or leave home without your American Express, MasterCard or Visa.

Moreover, you want the customer to use all of the features of the product, not just the most basic of them. Consider a new electronics product. Lengthy product manuals are not the way to go. In fact, they have been entirely discontinued over the years because customers don't have time for them (for some products, they are still available online). Rather, the key is designing the product to make sure that the consumer can immediately use it with little instruction and explore advanced features later on as they play around with the functionality. Apple's iPod got the jump on this with its minimalist packaging and intuitive design.

If you own an iPod, you may remember purchasing it and thinking, "Where's the big box and all the stuff that I'm expecting to be inside, like a full manual?" Of course the iPhone quickly followed suit with the very same style. Now other products, like Samsung's Galaxy smartphones and tablets, are using the same technique. But it only works when the product is well-thought-out and designed for intuitive navigation.

Finally, so-called lifestyle marketing is another way to arouse customers' interest and passions, and thus activate them. Instead of selling a product directly to customers, lifestyle marketing links the product to something the customer truly cares about in a personal way, something that makes them happy. For many, these areas are sports or entertainment.

HSBC, one of the largest banking and financial services organizations, bills itself as the "World's Local Bank" and uses personal banking in most of its markets. When you open a Premier account, with a minimum deposit of USD 150,000, you are assigned a relationship manager. That person is supposed to know you inside and out. I was referred to HSBC by a colleague who enthusiastically recommended their services after he had been invited to a dinner at one of the Nobu restaurants of Japanese "iron chef" Nobu Matsuhisa. His relationship manager had invited a dozen like-minded customers to mingle at the dinner. What a great way to activate the HSBC brand and elevate it from a mere cash depositor to a business enabler. When I considered opening an account, I met with the same relationship manager. When I mentioned my colleague's name and the Nobu event, he pulled a photo off his mobile phone, showing my colleague enjoying the Nobu experience. He immediately, but casually, inquired about my own interests and hobbies. A couple of weeks later, he called me on my mobile phone to invite me to a concert, based on our conversation. As you can see, lifestyle marketing is a great way to keep a brand on a customer's mind and to activate a brand and the emotions and values associated with it.

Customer activation is the first step of customer engagement. But you can go beyond simple interest and permanently raise a customer's passion for a brand by wholly and deeply engaging them in what you're offering. This gets us to Step 2, immersing the customer.

STEP 2: IMMERSING

The second step of the method is creating an all-out immersive brand experience. Immersion is not about getting attention, but about absorption. It is a mental and behavioral state character-ized by intense focus and seemingly effortless action. Immersion frequently happens to people playing video games, and I feel that we can learn some lessons from the producers of virtual reality.

Those who play will typically spend hours battling at an ar-cade, against their own computer or online in a multiplayer sce-nario, where other players join in from around the world. For many gamers, gaming is wickedly exciting and fosters a fanati-cal loyalty that few other products can match.[7] Whether playing Gears of War 3 on an Xbox360, Twisted Metal on a PlaySta-tion, or The Legend of Zelda: Skyward Sword on Wii's Motion Plus Sensor, gaming can be a great way to step out of normal reality and create a new one. Games run the gamut from educa-tional and child-friendly to very explicit adult versions of war, car chases, robbery and even simulated sex acts. Gamers spend a lot of money to get the games and the gear and even attend conven-tions to meet other gamers.

How is immersion accomplished here? First, there is a lot of multisensory stimulation and movement. Second, you are part of the action, an active participant. Third, the focus of your attention is on acting and reacting quickly.

To immerse customers, you therefore need complete control of the customer, of all of his or her senses and of the environment. You need to create an environment from which the customer cannot easily escape. Finally, you should consider a short time horizon, because immersion, while exciting for a while, can get exhausting over time.

In other words, you must own that trade show by blasting your messages everywhere. You must own YouTube for a brief stretch and do something spectacular there. Think like a marketer of Hollywood movies rather than a brand manager. When Hollywood launches a new movie, its studio spends most of its marketing budget within a very short time, right before the movie opens and during the first week, in order to create full immersion.

STEP 3: SHARING

The final step of the "Engagement" method is sharing. You can share all sorts of content and information about the company, online and offline, with anybody in the form of verbal information, images or video.

Of course, customers have shared content and information for a long time. For many decades, they have shared positive and negative experiences, recommended products and brands to friends and gone shopping together. What's new is the sheer amount of content that can be shared—easily and instantly—with anyone, in different forms. In vogue at the time of this writing are Google+, Facebook, Twitter, Flickr, Photobucket, Zoopy,

YouTube and countless blogs—but this will likely change as the old sites fall away and new ones replace them.

Illy, the Italian coffee company, has launched a campaign called "live HAPPilly" (sic!). Advertisements link the brand to customers' daily-life experiences by mentally priming them with a series of lifestyle buzzwords such as "drink, talk, meet, feel, dream, share, love." In addition, they have asked people to share with others how they live "HAPPilly" by submitting their happiness pictures online.

Sharing is not only important for B2C products, but also in B2B. Brainlab, a privately held company near Munich, Germany, is a market leader in image-guided technology. They develop and manufacture software for medical technology like brain scanners. There are 5,000 Brainlab systems installed in over 80 countries across Europe, Asia, Australia and North and South America.

The company has developed a cloud-based physician network that provides a secure environment for members to access, control and share diagnostic imaging anytime, anywhere. Moreover, via their website www.quentry.com, powerful, on-demand tools allow doctors to visualize the data, consult colleagues and synchronize work." Such sharing of visual information adds real value to doctors and hospitals," Stefan Vilsmeier, the CEO, told me. "It is an innovative way to create a B2B community." Most of the shared product information is textual and is still distributed via e-mail and via non-mobile devices (at least in the US). In more technologically advanced 3G and 4G mobile phone markets like Singapore, South Korea, Japan and other Asian as well as northern European markets, more sharing happens on smartphones, and the bulk of information is multimedia. This may soon change in the slower-adopting countries like the US, where the future is also likely to be mobile-based and multimedia.

Getting customers to share content makes them more likely to be buyers and repeat customers, and even prompts them to recruit other customers. Yet, there continues to be a cost barrier to the customer—in both time and mental resources—which is why sharing is an important indicator of customer engagement.

As mobile communications gain further ground, content sharing will happen more, and customers will decide while they shop and while they consume, rather than afterwards. As sharing becomes more directly linked to the commercial point of contact, it will be increasingly important for companies to reduce the time and mental costs involved in sharing content about their products and brands with other customers.

Why do we share content online? In the summer of 2011, the Customer Insight Group of the *New York Times* presented the results of a survey on "the psychology of sharing."[9] The most important, if not particularly surprising, finding: sharing (as a key step of customer engagement) is about relationships between the company and among customers. Specifically, we share because we want to bring valuable content to others. We want to get the word out and we define ourselves based on the content we share.

The *New York Times* team recommends that to get customers to share more, the company needs to establish trust with its customers. Plus, content shouldn't be too heavily branded: it should have entertaining elements and be immediately relevant to the customer.[10]

In a sense, online customer engagement is continuing an offline conversation in a different medium. But that does not do justice to the significance of this new form of engagement.

What is being said online is mostly public. In fact, it is publicity, even though it may come under the disguise of intimacy. It often reaches a global audience. Perhaps the Net Promoter Score question should be updated for the digital age, referring to this extended community of friends and the world.

From a marketing perspective, online customer engagement efforts should differ from offline. Online content needs to be more transparent, open, direct, less planned and less corporate and commercial. Businesses are losing the power to manipulate their customers in the old Orwellian "big brother" style. Now and in the future, companies will need to market to us, or rather with us, in a more human way. That will make all customers happier.

To conclude this chapter, I'd like to consider customer engagement with lingerie. How can you engage customers with a clothing category that is so private and that most people never get to see? We can learn a lesson or two about customer engagement from the marketing that takes place in this category.

VICTORIA'S SECRET:
ENGAGING WITH LINGERIE

Lingerie is a curious thing. For centuries underwear was all about functionality and comfort—and cotton. As a result of clever marketing, more and more women are now becoming deeply engaged with the category, even obsessed by the fantasy that can surround their wearing of lingerie.

According to the apparel and textile information website just-style, the average European or North American woman's wardrobe has between five and eight bras and up to ten pairs of panties.[10] On average, she will buy two bras and five pairs of panties per year. Hard-core lingerie devotees, on the other hand, will have considerably larger collections. Some shop for lingerie several times per year.

Lingerie shopping is therefore a big business: just-style's global market review of lingerie and intimate apparel estimates the global lingerie market will be worth USD 32 billion by 2016 (up from USD 29 billion in 2009).[11] The annual sales of Victoria's Secret alone, the leading US brand, surpass USD 5 billion.

But these numbers are just numbers and only tell one part of the story. The real story is how lingerie can engage women to a point where they are deeply immersed with the product or brand. Victoria's Secret is truly a champion in accomplishing this task. It has a lot to do with engaging the customer with variety-style product marketing, original brand extensions, flagship stores, oversized billboards and an innovative online and TV presence. Let's consider each of these marketing tools in more detail.

THE PRODUCT

Lingerie comes in cotton, Lycra, silk, spandex, rayon and many other materials. The technology and fabrics of the 1970s led to more intricate products like the Wonderbra with its "push up and plunge" effect.[12] In the early 1980s, padded and underwire bras were top sellers, and lingerie offered women a soft, sensual style that was often meant to be partially seen. Now there are gel, air-filled, backless bras; sexy thongs; pouty teddies; and a huge variety of anything from "granny panties" to fetish wear. At Victoria's Secret, there are push-up bras, wireless bras, and strapless bras (for the top) as well as briefs, thongs and so-called boyshorts (for the bottom). There are basics, lingerie-style swimwear, yoga and loungewear. Names can be revealing, too. Think of Victoria

Secret's "Ultra-Push Up," guaranteeing two additional bra sizes "instantly." Or the 2011 newly launched "Showstopper." Tag line: "Show nothing but your shape." All of these choices allow women to be whoever they choose. They can be innocent or seductive, frumpy or sultry. They can remain themselves or transform into an alter-ego.

BRAND EXTENSIONS

Consider Victoria's Secret "Pink," launched in late 2004. Pink has been a runaway success that engaged a new group of customers. Positioned at 18- to 22-year-olds, tweens, high school and college students, Pink has exactly these girls snapping up lingerie, loungewear, sleepwear, coats, backpacks, bedding and even luggage in every shade of pink (including thongs and more intimate styles) that come in "100 playful prints and colors" with catchy slogans like "Pink Party Girl," "Kiss Me at Midnight," "Keep Me Warm" and "Hit the Road." [13] The company, which traditionally sold to older women, moved seamlessly into an untapped younger market.

Today, Pink is a USD 1 billion brand. It's no secret that if you engage a younger demographic and make them happy, they will tell their friends and further drive product sales. If the company doesn't let them down at some point, the young customers will become older customers as they mature with the brand. [14]

FLAGSHIP STORES

In 2002, the company revamped more than 1,000 stores and created new flagship stores. CEO Leslie Wexner said the overhaul was initiated to make Victoria's Secret a more upscale brand in consumers' minds, to boost the racy factor without cheapening the store's image.[15] Traditionally, Victoria's Secret stores were soft and feminine; the new store designs, in contrast, were overtly sexier. When the 2005 grand opening of a Victoria's Secret store in Virginia featured the "Dirty Little Secrets" line, shoppers were shocked to see scantily clad mannequins in poses suggestive of lesbianism and sadomasochism. A group of unhappy parents protested loudly, thus prompting store management to tone down the display.

THE BILLBOARDS

From New York's Times Square to London's Piccadilly Circus to the center of Seoul and beyond, oversized billboards displaying lingerie contribute their share to the lingerie industry in dollar volume and in emotional expression. The logic goes like this: if the ads are deemed too "sexually suggestive," so much the better for publicity. In 2009, a Victoria's Secret mobile billboard campaign showed close-up images of model Heidi Klum.[16] Some would criticize it as tacky and inappropriate; others would point out that the campaign got a whole lot of free publicity.

ONLINE (AND TV) PRESENCE

Lingerie sites are creative and fun to explore. The Facebook site of Victoria's Secret features wall photos and event videos to launch its new Perfect One full-coverage bra, all meant to draw in, engage and retain their customers. Victoria's Secret also runs online fashion shows and has produced shows for TV. However, this is not without controversy. According to the CBS promo at the time, the show that featured "the most beautiful women in the world wearing the very latest in Victoria's Secret lingerie" was often swamped before and after airing with calls and e-mails about the inappropriate content. It will be interesting to watch how the issue plays out as the company moves into Latin America, Kuwait and the United Arab Emirates.

CONCLUSION

Whether it's Coke or Victoria's Secret, customer engagement is crucial for getting customers to buy and buy again and again, beyond just feeling good or connected to their values. In this chapter, we have discussed the "Engagement" method to achieve this goal. You can use the method to activate your customers, immerse them in an experience and get them to share it.

By now, you are equipped with three general methods for making customers happy. In the next chapter, I will explore how the framework and methods presented thus far can be implemented, through product design, events, social media and other devices.

6

HAPPINESS TOUCHPOINTS

So you have decided to take customers' happiness seriously. You want to create small pleasures in their lives and make them feel good. You want to connect to their values and, through your products or services, add meaning to their lives. Moreover, you want to engage them. As we have already seen, there are three methods for accomplishing these goals.

- To add pleasure to customers' lives you can use the "Feel Good" method. This requires you to enrich your customers' experience, get them to savor it and then expand the experience in order to repeatedly surround them with pleasurable moments.
- To add meaning to your customers' lives through your products and services, you can use the "Values-and-Meaning" method. Identify personal values that are important to customers, get them to focus on these values and place your offer in a broader context.

• Finally, the "Engagement" method can activate customers, immerse them fully in the experience and then induce them to share the happiness experience with others.

How can you successfully implement these three methods? What "thinking style" should you adopt to create pleasure, meaning and engagement? What are the key happiness touchpoints at which to implement these methods?

Typically, pleasure as a goal—that is, delivering those small, enjoyable, surprising moments that make people feel good—is best accomplished when you think like a designer. Many positive experiences happen during consumption, when the customer actually uses the product. If you design the product the right way and if it looks good, you are creating many daily pleasures for your customers. Also, the retail and shopping environment is a key pleasure touchpoint: designing the right retail environment; treating customers in a special way at the point of purchase; and creating an environment that stirs their desire to buy—all of these will make customers feel good. Finally, if you design your through-sales and after-sales service appropriately, you can deliver numerous niceties and touches that differentiate your offer. The key is to think like a designer when you create products, retail environments and service maps. These touchpoints should all be executed in a creative, innovative way.

When meaning is your goal, you need to think like a cultural anthropologist, analyzing the values of your customers and deciding which signs and symbols will be relevant to them in a social and communal setting. As for pleasure happiness, your product and core service is a key touchpoint, but it needs to be used for something other than pleasure. Consider, for example, the consumer value trends (protection of the environment, simplicity and monetary value) that we discussed in chapter 4. Plan the product and service in such a way that its essence is compatible with these values. Moreover, plan meaningful communications, including messages and images, because they are important signs and signals in meaning creation and in conveying that your company and its brands stand for such values. Additionally, your company must be a responsible community member; your corporate social responsibility (CSR) cannot be an afterthought. CSR must be at the core of your organization, an essential touchpoint for meaning creation.

Finally, for engagement happiness, consider yourself as part of a production team that co-produces the engagement show. Once again, the core product and service play an important role. However, the company must also be open to customer suggestions: it must view product and service design as a co-creation process. Another key engagement touchpoint is events. They are a great implementation tool for activating and immersing customers in brand experiences, and if they are produced in a spectacular way, they will be shared and create effective word-of-mouth both offline and online. Finally, social media are an essential touchpoint for engaging entire customer networks. In sum, engagement happiness is best accomplished through co-creation, primarily through events and social media.

Let's take a look at exactly how you can implement happiness campaigns by examining the most important touchpoints for each type of happiness.

```
┌─────────────────────────────────────────────────────┐
│         TOUCHPOINTS FOR PLEASURE HAPPINESS            │
│              • Aesthetic Product Design               │
│              • Experiential Retailing                 │
│              • Service with a Twist                   │
│                                                       │
│         TOUCHPOINTS FOR MEANING HAPPINESS             │
│              • Product (and Brand) Essence            │
│              • Authentic Communications               │
│              • CSR on a Mission                       │
│                                                       │
│        TOUCHPOINTS FOR ENGAGEMENT HAPPINESS           │
│              • Co-creation with a Stake               │
│              • Splash Events                          │
│              • The Social Media of the Moment         │
└─────────────────────────────────────────────────────┘
```

FIGURE 6. HAPPINESS TOUCHPOINTS

TOUCHPOINTS FOR PLEASURE HAPPINESS

For most companies, product design and aesthetics, the retailing environment, and the service experience are the three most critical touchpoints for pleasure happiness. These three types of touchpoints are all interactional and yield immediate benefits; they can provide solutions during purchase and consumption situations and therefore make customers feel good.

However, not every type of product design, retail environment or service results in pleasure. Products must be designed a certain way, retail environments must be constructed and managed a certain way and service must be executed appropriately to be enjoyable. What you need is what I call "aesthetic product design," "experiential retailing" and "service with a twist."

AESTHETIC PRODUCT DESIGN

How can a product design promote pleasure? As we saw in chapter 3, W Hotels has numerous design components in its properties that, when combined, create what my co-author and I in 1997 called "marketing aesthetics," in our book of the same name.[1] Product design creates pleasure when it delivers more than functionality, when it has aesthetic value. Don't get me wrong: functionality is important; products must work. But it is the aesthetics that largely contribute to pleasure happiness. Aesthetics must appeal to customers, surprise them and intrigue them. Only then will it make them feel good and happy. Let me illustrate my point with an unusual product made by a company that we already encountered earlier, the Dutch electronics and appliances conglomerate Philips.

Philips' Intimate Massagers

Philips's product line of intimate massagers was first launched in the UK, targeting heterosexual couples. Here is what you can read about it on the Amazon UK website:

> *"We all know a satisfying sex life between partners makes for a happy couple. We also know that a couple's intimate relationship is often the first thing to suffer from the stress and pressures of modern times. The intimate massager addresses this vital, but often neglected, aspect of our lives. It offers a new way for couples to explore each other's desires and take their intimate relationship to a new level."*[2]

Clearly, the product design, aesthetics and name are crucial so that we don't confuse the "intimate massagers," (or "sensual massagers," as Philips also calls them) with what they actually are—vibrators. This allows the product to be sold in pharmacy chains and department stores rather than at sex shops.

At the official Philips online shop in the UK, I read the following:

"Distinct design for his and her erogenous zones. This set is perfect for the two of you to stimulate each other's erogenous zones at the same time. There are two massagers, one for him, one for her, each with a stimulating spot to give your partner pleasure."[3]

Are you curious yet? The product description on the site comes with a series of enlargeable product images, a demonstration video and surprisingly explicit language to describe the male and female massagers, respectively. For example,

"The curves of the male massager are shaped for his most intimate contours, enhancing erotic pleasure. Slowly brush the wider surface of the massagers, for instance, up the inside of the thigh or gently along the penis. The rounded tips are perfect for teasing in more focused ways and locations, such as around the nipple or between the genital and rectal area."

The massager designed to please her also boasts a unique design.

"The female massager is specially shaped to stimulate and please her. The tip is the area of the massager that vibrates, allowing you to stimulate her erogenous zones. Try a relaxing pulse on the labia or hold the tip of the massager downwards to titillate the clitoris."

Those Philips engineers really paid attention to the details of the product design and aesthetics. The products look more like Zen stones than traditional vibrators. Both products use "sensual materials," and have a "gentle sound" (46db on average). They can be used together with lubricants and are "splash proof" and "easy to clean." They come with multiple vibration modes and intensities (referred to as "Glow," "Wave," "Heartbeat" and "Thrill"). As with a laptop, voltage is adjustable from 100 to 240v, allowing you to take the massagers on trips! There is also a "discreet charging case" for cordless charging and storage: "You can just leave it on your nightstand! No one will ever know what you use it for . . ."

At the launch in 2008, Philips estimated the annual market for intimate massagers to be above USD 1 billion (USD 130 million in the UK alone) and expected their product to contribute an additional USD 120 million.[4] Research indicated that 42 percent of couples in the UK used some sort of marital aid and of those who did not, 35 percent were willing to try it.

As this case shows, attention to detail in product design and aesthetics is important. For the Philips product line, the physical functionality, ergonomics and certain perceptual features that transformed the product from a "naughty" or taboo product to a "lifestyle" device have made the Philips Intimate Massager one of the most satisfying sex toys for couples.

Of course, the competition doesn't sit still. The "Duet" by Crave is another new, multispeed waterproof vibrator that entered the market in 2011. The Duet is the size of a flash drive; it is rechargeable via a USB drive, lasts about four hours on a single charge, and includes 8 GB of storage. It's quite possibly the world's sexiest data storage device. Designer Ti Chang explains on YouTube:

> *"Sexuality is unique and diverse to a lot of women. So we spent time listening and understanding what's important to them . . . They were afraid of buying batteries because they were afraid that people would look at them as if they were buying batteries for their vibrators."*[5]

She stresses that it's better for the environment, too.

There are many other examples of how slight, yet significant, changes in design and aesthetics can lead to major changes in daily customer happiness. German car manufacturers originally sneered at Americans who demanded coffee-cup holders next to the driver's seat. None of these German engineers had wanted the coffee-cup holders installed because cup holders in a car did not fit with their sense of aesthetics. Yet, over time, coffee-cup holders have proved to add a little extra pleasure to customers' lives, so these car companies finally gave in.

In the next chapter, we will examine a new digital camera with a simple feature—a screen on both the front and the back of the camera—and how it adds pleasure to people's lives. There are numerous other design opportunities to be discovered. But we can only discover them if we truly focus on delivering customer happiness.

EXPERIENTIAL RETAILING

In a retail environment, there are many different factors to consider. One factor is location. Is the store in a city? Which part of the city? Is it in a mall or on a shopping street? Also, what type of retailer is it (department store, supermarket, discount store)? There are also many in-store factors, like the atmosphere, sales people, product displays and others. But it is not just any form of retailing that can create pleasure and happiness; it demands a specific approach.

If you are focused on pleasure happiness, retailing matters. It matters where the products are sold (location), what the surroundings are like (type of retailing) and how products are sold (in-store factors). The key to creating small, pleasurable moments for customers is what's known as experiential retailing. This new type of retailing, which came to prominence in the first decade of this century, has three defining characteristics.

First, experiential retailing provides not just an environment for buying. It is also an environment for entertaining the customer. There are things happening in the store. For example: enjoyable product demonstrations; good music, perhaps even a live band; and other events or programs.

Second, experiential retailing is not just an assembly of products. Rather, there is a theme. The theme may be the brand and its various products, as in a flagship store. It may be a focus on a certain kind of customer interest or lifestyle: trendy luxury fashion, outdoor sports or a kitchen theme. Or it may be a certain product line or a "special sale," as in a pop-up store that is set up temporarily.

Third, experiential retailing is a soft sell and thus quite unlike traditional retailing. You are not being bothered by pushy sales people and discount displays. Instead, you are seduced, drawn in to stay, and if the sale happens, so much the better. Incidentally, when it happens, it is likely to be at a higher price point.

As part of the executive workshops I conduct in New York, I offer an experiential retailing tour. We go to the Abercrombie & Fitch flagship store on Fifth Avenue, to Whole Foods Market at Columbus Circle or to one of the Bed, Bath and Beyond or Williams-Sonoma stores. We may check out a new pop-up store in SoHo or in the Meatpacking District. At night, we examine other benchmarks and new ideas for experiential retailing—so we look for inspiration at W Times Square or a theme restaurant. After all, new hotels and eateries are, in themselves, very experiential. They don't just serve food; they entertain. They have a theme and they soft-sell to get you to try additional items (such as a massage, dessert or after-dinner drink).

Let's visit an experiential store together and notice the entertaining, thematic and soft-sell elements that seem to add pleasure for visitors.

The National Geographic Experience

National Geographic is no longer just a yellow-edged magazine showing topless indigenous men and women. It isn't only TV documentaries either. Now the organization is going further afield to bring the world in which we live to you and to others.

Enter the National Geographic retail stores. They most certainly follow our three defining characteristics of experiential retailing.

They are exciting, mysterious and entertaining. From the minute you walk inside, the mood is distinct. Dark walls and ceilings with high-end mood lighting take the customer, psychologically, into a different world.

They have a theme: their stores are all about adventure and experience.

And there's the soft sell. There are separate zones to browse National Geographic books, videos or guides, an area with dramatic and beautifully framed (and very pricey) photographs, branded clothing, travel accessories (bags, binoculars, watches, hats) as well as home furnishings (think Indiana Jones meets Martha Stewart), and even a kid's zone with educational and fun toys. The company running these outlets by license, Worldwide Retail Store, also organizes regular public lectures by well-known explorers, authors and photographers and offers free film screenings. All of this is done to keep customers returning as often as possible.

My co-author, Glenn van Zutphen, loves the National Geographic experience; in fact, he insisted that we describe it in this book. After seeing the Singapore store while we were working on this book, I happily concurred. My favorite aspect of the Singapore store was a climate-controlled chamber.[6] Once inside the glass room, the temperature quickly drops to 1.5 degrees Celsius, allowing the customer to see how their tropical-weight clothing or cold weather expedition gear (for sale in the store, of course) might work in real-life winter conditions. A fan in the chamber also simulates wind chill, a key factor in body heat loss. Customers can see the change in their body temperatures on a screen linked to a thermal camera. This is truly a great experience in sultry Singapore, where the temperature rarely goes below 27 degrees Celsius!

By the way, Glenn is not only an accomplished writer and media person. He loves the outdoors. At one point during the writing of this book, I could not track him down for three days. He had flown to Borneo to do a two-day climb up Mount Kinabalu where temperatures are a balmy 20–25 degrees Celsius at the base and plunge to near freezing at the peak. (For me, the climate-controlled chamber at the National Geographic store was enough of an experience).

The National Geographic experience appeals to customers on many levels: great ambiance, quality products, a vast assortment of interesting things to look at, aspirational travel and adventure, music (often a Putumayo soundtrack) and a café where you can sit and drink in the experience.

The stores are part natural history museum and part flea market, as well as part travel clothing store, library, art gallery and toy store. With seven stores now open (London, Madrid, Andorra, Malaga, Palma de Mallorca, Kuala Lumpur and Singapore), there are plans for stores in 80 countries.[7] Of course, the merchandise is not cheap, but the target market is upscale, eco-conscious, globally minded travelers (and armchair travelers like me), a demographic segment that values quality and is willing to pay, especially if the merchandise is presented as part of experiential retailing.

SERVICE WITH A TWIST

In addition to aesthetic product design and experiential retailing, you need one other distinct touchpoint to induce pleasure: service. True customer happiness demands not generic service or even generically good service, but service with a twist.

Many developed economies are service economies. As a result, over the last several decades, service has become increasingly professional, constructed, and planned. The best service you're likely to get today is standardized and consistent. It is data- and information-rich but increasingly automated and impersonal. Such service is usually better in many ways than the face-to-face service offered in the old days, when companies had no stored data on customers, and started from square one every time. But if we believe the feedback given through surveys, our expectations have risen correspondingly.

Because of the data and logistics revolution, which has forced companies to focus on consistency, information and the need to save costs through automation, many have lost the opportunities to surprise customers through creating pleasurable moments. If you want customers to feel good and experience bliss through service, you should offer service with a twist. Remember W Hotel's mantra of Whatever/Whenever. That's what I am talking about. Here is another example.

Crutchfield

Setting up electronic devices can be a frustrating experience. When you are working in a corporation, you can get help from the IT department. For your private purchases, you may have to get it elsewhere.

When I decided to set up a new surround sound system in my home, I was terrified by the complexity of the task: the speakers, receivers and cables, which to connect, where and how. Thankfully, I called the call center at crutchfield.com, and the representative took the time to simplify the task and walk me through the set-up process. He spent 40 minutes on the phone helping me sort out the complicated (so it seemed to me) procedure and choose the right components. When the equipment arrived, I found a handwritten note attached: "If you have any more questions, call back and ask for me. Pete." I was pleasantly surprised!

The Virginia-based company is known for this sort of service—service with a twist. Bill Crutchfield started the company in 1974 as a car stereo business; sales during the first year were bad. To find out why, he mailed a questionnaire to several hundred customers. They replied that they were intimidated by the thought of installing a car stereo. So the company realized it could differentiate itself by offering not just a great product, but also exceptional service through a customer hot line that provided step-by-step instructions on how to install the stereo.

Although purchasing of such products nowadays occurs mostly online, there are still a lot of people (like me) who need and appreciate this kind of service. In fact, quite a few online companies have come to realize that personalized and exceptional service is important. For example, Tony Hsieh started a now-famous online business, Zappos, and later sold it to amazon.com. He wrote a book called *Delivering Happiness* about his business experience, which explores the relationship between service and happiness in his business.[8]

TOUCHPOINTS FOR MEANING HAPPINESS

When your happiness campaign focuses on values to create meaning happiness, you need to use some different touchpoints. The product is still critical, though in a different way. Communications and CSR can be key implementation tools to provide customers with valuable meaning. You can use all three touchpoints to make customer values salient and help customers focus on their values.

Yet, similar to pleasure touchpoints, not every type of product design or communication or CSR will make the cut for meaning happiness. It is essential to focus on the essence of the product or brand; you need authentic communication strategies and CSR campaigns that are not an afterthought but an organic part of a broader mission.

PRODUCT (AND BRAND) ESSENCE

Remember the yoga craze in chapter 4? There wasn't much of a product there, but every surrounding product that I described (the mats, the towels, the clothing) reinforced the core essence of yoga as a spiritual way to gain insight and to breathe in . . . breathe out.

Similarly, an environmental product had better be green! A certain look and feel may reinforce it. But the product ingredients, where and how the product is sourced as well as the production and delivery process, must also be right; otherwise the aesthetic is perceived as fake, and customers will react negatively.

If efficiency is the value, the essence of the product or service, whether it is a PDA or a hotel, had better be efficient. Thus, for the PDA user experience, it must take only one click, not three, to get to the appointment calendar. For the hotel design, easy access to electrical outlets is important to the business traveler. No crawling around the room should be required.

A brand as a whole, together with its combination of various products and/or services, needs to know its own essence in order to relate to values and create meaning. Look at the Virgin brand and how founder Richard Branson represents its essence.

The Essence of Virgin

There really isn't anything that Sir Richard Branson can't do. At least that's my impression from having watched his eclectic career over several decades. Talk about a guy that knows how to achieve while creating meaning for his own life and for anyone who chooses to patronize any of his many businesses.

On the face of it, it may seem as if his Virgin Group has no identifiable brand essence, as discussed above. Its businesses range from music to mobile phones to credit cards to airlines and trains to insurance. What is the core essence of this corporate brand? Actually, the essence may be the Richard Branson brand itself.

I was interviewed for Bloomberg's "Game Changer" series and was asked if Virgin is not only a brand, but Richard Branson himself. I answered "absolutely" and said that Branson represents the Virgin brand's essence very well because he understands branding and knows how to brand himself. I recalled a funny encounter with him when we met World Business Forum in New York run by HSM, a conference organizer. Directing the Center on Global Brand Leadership at Columbia Business School, I was introduced to him as "the brand professor." He smiled and asked politely whether I could tell him a little bit about branding.

Perhaps the seemingly crazy career twists and turns are, in fact, the essence of who Branson is and what Virgin Group does as a brand. Some of his biographers note that business partners have routinely advised him over the years not to dilute his brand by straying away from the core businesses. But, as we all know, he does it anyway, believing that if the Virgin Group offers a useful product at a good price with great customer service (and a dose of his considerable promotional abilities), they will succeed no matter what the industry is. Branson's entrepreneurial quest is to consistently shake things up, push the limits and exceed expectations. That's why customers value the Virgin brand, why they admire Branson and why his values inspire them.

So now, after starting Virgin Airlines and Virgin America in the US, Branson is pushing Virgin into space with Virgin Galactic. Based at Spaceport America in New Mexico, Virgin Galactic is attempting to make private, suborbital space travel available to everyone for the first time. Virgin Galactic will own and operate privately built spaceships, based on their proprietary SpaceShipOne technology. The company is investing more than USD 200 million in the development of the new SpaceShipTwo system and believes that the system and its future derivatives may be the source of scientific, commercial and space tourism. In fact, NASA has already chosen Virgin Galactic to provide flight opportunities for engineers, technologists and scientific researchers to take technology payloads into space.[9] It's the first time the US space agency has contracted with a commercial partner to provide flights into space on a suborbital spacecraft.

The three-plus-hour ride will cost USD 200,000. The actual time in weightless space will last about five minutes for the two pilots and six passengers on each flight. As of this writing, Virgin Galactic won't confirm when the commercial flights will start, but many test flights have already been done. Interestingly, more than 400 individuals have reportedly signed up as of early 2011, paying deposits of USD 20,000.[10]

AUTHENTIC COMMUNICATIONS

As we saw in chapter 4, it's hard to get communications right when values are involved. Consumers often perceive communications (advertising, public relations, even some new media campaigns set up by companies and agencies) as inherently manipulative and do not trust them as information devices. They view communications with suspicion and cynicism.

To be seen as truly authentic, "real" and "believable," a company must show extra effort, be incredibly consistent in its communications, and stick to its position, even running an "anticampaign." Social psychologists have called this "minority influence"—sticking to your point of view even when there is a potentially high cost to pay.[11]

In sum, being truly authentic and real is tough. Unilever's Dove brand succeeded in doing so, but it also faced intense scrutiny over its Campaign for Real Beauty.

How Real Is "Real Beauty"?

When it launched the campaign in 2004, Unilever's Dove brand hit a home run, as they say in baseball. The Campaign for Real Beauty turned out to be a unique kind of "anti-campaign," focusing on average women with average looks instead of the perfectly primped, glamorous models that have been pimped in advertising for decades.

The idea behind Real Beauty was to celebrate natural beauty and inspire women to be confident and comfortable with the way they look. Ogilvy & Mather, the ad agency involved, chose British portrait and fashion photographer Rankin, who is known for his work with non-professional models, to do the shoots.[12] For Dove, featuring these women was seen as enormously bold and empowering.

I included the campaign in my 2007 book, *Big Think Strategy*. After the book was published, the Dove product group called me in to ask for innovative ideas.[13] The all-women team put me on the hot seat right in the center of the room, and said, "Professor, give us *your* big ideas." I soon realized that their thinking was well ahead of mine.

Connecting with consumers in new ways was a hallmark of the campaign. One billboard asked viewers to call a toll-free number to vote on whether the women pictured were "fat or fab." Results were posted on the board in real time. It worked for a while, but eventually the "fat" votes won—oops . . .

That mishap aside, the campaign worked brilliantly for years, garnering many awards and lots of free press, and becoming the industry standard (Baiersdorf's Nivea brand launched a similar campaign), creating a real and lasting conversation about how society and the cosmetic and fashion industries shape the concept of beauty. It also increased Dove's market share—quite an achievement for a mature category brand.

Famous YouTube ads such as "Dove Evolution" and "Dove Onslaught" demonstrated authentic communication as the former went head-to-head with beauty advertising and the latter commented on the negative effects of the beauty industry on young girls. Each went viral, telling a story that made clear points about the evils of the way traditional advertising has portrayed women and pressured them into being someone they're not.

"Dove Evolution," which got 13.5 million hits on YouTube, presented a 45-second time-lapse video on how a model is made up, styled, photographed and retouched to look acceptable to the art director. It's chilling to see how they transform someone to look like another person. The kicker line: "No wonder our perception of beauty is distorted."

In the 2007 follow-up video, "Dove Onslaught," the ad harshly criticized how distorted beauty images encouraged eating disorders and other problems with young women. The tag line: "Talk to your daughter before the beauty industry does."

So why did Dove, in early 2011, tell its ad agency to stop the Campaign for Real Beauty in favor of something "less preachy," as reported on wonderbranding.com?[14]

Perhaps the change occurred because Real Beauty's authenticity over the years became tarnished and overshadowed by what some critics called hypocrisy. On the one hand, the Real Beauty campaign preached global self-esteem for women, urging them to be happy with themselves. On the other hand, consumers saw that Unilever still markets thigh-firming cream, wrinkle-reducing serum, skin-lightening cream (in Asia and India) and Slim-Fast (in the UK), in whose ads women are told they need to lose weight to fit into cute dresses. The Campaign for a Commercial-Free Childhood blasted Unilever's AXE brand men's deodorant, which routinely uses young women in sexually charged ads. Each time I moderated a discussion session with a Unilever participant, there was at least one person in the audience who pointed out these inconsistencies.

On top of that, in a 2008 *New Yorker* profile, a photo editor claimed to have retouched photos used in the Campaign for Real Beauty.[15] This raised the question in the minds of some consumers: How real *is* Real Beauty? The full extent of the changes was not revealed, and it should be noted that many advertising execs of both genders thought there was nothing wrong with giving the photos a little help as long as the basic look was not changed. But this revelation undermined the "natural" premise of what Dove was trying to say to women around the world.

Keep an eye out for their new campaign. It is reported to steer away from body image toward helping women feel confident in their appearance through "fun messaging," which may indicate a shift from values-and-meaning marketing toward pleasure marketing. It's believed the new campaign will also return to using professional models.

CORPORATE SOCIAL RESPONSIBILITY ON A MISSION

Besides product, brand essence and authentic communications, corporate social responsibility (CSR) is important for value creation and reinforcement. CSR campaigns relate a company to a much broader set of constituents than their existing customers

(B2B or B2C) by extending concern to additional stakeholders (employees, communities, etc.).

Great CSR campaigns are not just about giving money. They can define the purpose of a company by helping to achieve societal goals, together with staff and customers. They can make employees proud and other stakeholders happy. Such CSR initiatives, and the people who run them, are, literally, on a mission. Here is an example of such a campaign.

Yuhan-Kimberly: "Keep Korea Green"[16]

The Yuhan Corporation started in 1926 as a pharmaceutical business, making it one of the oldest companies in Korea. In 1970, Yuhan entered into a joint venture with Kimberly-Clark. The new Yuhan-Kimberly factory produced toilet paper, facial tissues and feminine napkins. Sales in the first year were a modest 300 million won. But as the company tapped into an emerging Korean middle class and its demand for paper-based family products, the need for more specialized paper products expanded. By 1994, three factories contributed to annual sales of KRW 268 billion. By 2007, when I co-authored a business case about the company with Dae Ryun Chang, a Korean professor at Yonsei University, Yuhan-Kimberly was so successful that it reached net sales of KRW 905 billion and its business portfolio consisted of ten sectors. The most successful products continued to be all paper products: baby diapers, facial and bathroom tissue and feminine napkins. Those products had captured about 80 percent of the company's total revenues during the previous three years.

From the start, Yuhan-Kimberly was an organization that focused consciously on broad social and societal values. Founder Il-han New's management philosophy was that "profit-seeking is worthwhile only when it results not just in individual wealth but also in national prosperity." As such, over the years, the company has offered programs like an employee stock ownership plan, sponsorship of a technical high school and boarding school and generous gifts to charity. Yuhan-Kimberly's Family Friendly Management programs and policies included flexible work schedules, gender equality, maternity protection, an employee assistance program and volunteer opportunities. The flexible work schedule program allowed employees time to rest, enroll in work-related or lifelong educational programs and spend more time with their families. The costs of the lifelong educational programs for the employees and their dependents were subsidized by Yuhan-Kimberly. These programs not only resonated with employees, but also with the public, who started to see Yuhan-Kimberly as an employer that was truly concerned about its internal and external communities.

Most importantly, soon after the company expanded into the paper business, Yuhan-Kimberly tried to fulfill its environmental responsibilities by using natural resources as carefully as possible, reducing energy consumption to alleviate climate change and leading the industry in employing new environmentally friendly technology in its manufacturing processes.

In 1984 Yuhan-Kimberly officially began its green campaign. To many, it did not make sense that Yuhan-Kimberly, as a large health and hygiene company, would start such an environmental initiative. Stakeholders, including its major shareholders, business partners, some of its top executives and even the Ministry of Forestry, were dumbfounded. There was also grumbling from some of the company's employees, who were asked to plant trees but felt they had better things to do.

Ironically, even at that time, South Koreans were well aware of the need for reforestation. Thirty-six years of Japanese rule in the early part of the twentieth century and the Korean War in the 1950s had devastated much of the country's forests. Moreover, the industrialization of South Korea during the 1960s and 1970s had taken place without much consideration for the environment. As a result, in the early 1980s only one-third of South Korea's mountains (comprising 65 percent of all land), had been reforested. Despite the misgivings of those inside and outside of Yuhan-Kimberly, the CEO and top management considered it a moral obligation to vigorously pursue the "Keep Korea Green" campaign. There was a collective sense that if they did not do something, no one would. "People can care and talk about societal problems all they like," Eun-Wook Lee, Yuhan-Kimberly's Vice President of Corporate Communications, told me, "but will have little power to effect change. That is why companies must play a more proactive role to promote societal progress and make a difference."

The program started with a reforestation program under the slogan "Sharing a vision: love for trees." This phrase was designed to restore the original look and conditions of some key sites and also to inspire South Koreans to love trees. From 1984 to 2008, Yuhan-Kimberly planted and nurtured over 21 million trees on 7,533 hectares of public and state-owned land.

The second phase began in 1998 when Yuhan-Kimberly turned "Keep Korea Green" into a national effort focused on nurturing trees instead of just planting them. The company also provided environmental awareness education for South Korean kids with students from 2,012 schools participating in this program.

In the third phase, the company extended the campaign to North Korea, China and Mongolia. After the Korean War, North Korea cleared its mountains for farming, leaving them ravaged. The resulting bad soil led to chronic food shortages in North Korea. Since 1999, Yuhan-Kimberly has visibly strived to help the reforestation. Part of its plan centered on the famous Mt. Keumkang, an area of immense pride to both North and South Koreans.

The company also tackled an important regional problem: each year around March, Koreans suffer from the effects of yellow dust blowing into their country from northern Asia. Coughing, fever, sore throats, runny noses and sinus problems are some of the effects of this annual problem. Yellow dust is also a serious environmental concern in China, and desertification in North Asia is a contributing factor. In recognition of this problem, Yuhan-Kimberly helped to plant over 2.6 million trees in China and Mongolia to prevent further desertification in those countries.

Let's look at some outcome measures of the campaign. According to a consumer survey on corporate image in 2002, the company ranked first among South Korean companies for goodwill, trust and contribution to society. Also, a study in 2007 conducted by Gallup Korea showed that Yuhan-Kimberly was perceived as the most eco-friendly corporation in South Korea, beating out much bigger companies such as Samsung, LG and Hyundai. Yuhan-Kimberly was also perceived as outperforming many of its rivals in terms of workplace environment quality.

Furthermore, a 1999 internal study on the link between the "Keep Korea Green" campaign and brand equity showed positive correlations between the campaign and both corporate and individual brand-equity measures. Finally, a study by the LG

Economic Institute showed that almost 90 percent of Korean consumers were willing to pay a premium for the products of environmentally friendly companies.

In sum, Yuhan-Kimberly has successfully identified and focused the attention of Korean citizens on a value that is important to them and used the social context of the environmental issue to position itself as a value-focused leader. But it has not all been smooth sailing for the company, despite the efforts they've made to be a good corporate citizen and sensitive to their customer's values. The "Keep Korea Green" initiative, for example, has been criticized by environmentalist and civic groups who continue to see the campaign as a cynical attempt to compensate for the serious environmental damage caused by both the production and disposal of paper products.

TOUCHPOINTS FOR ENGAGEMENT HAPPINESS

Finally, key touchpoints for engagement happiness include co-creation of the product, event marketing and social media. All three have in common the need for a community of customers with various levels of involvement. They are triggers for community building and engagement. The strategic question is how much of and what type of community a company aspires to create. Generally speaking, the greater the community, the higher the engagement with customers.

Co-creation typically engages already-active customers—that is, those who are already part of a community. Event marketing can engage both active and passive customers and have both of them participate in a temporary, face-to-face community. Social media can create large communities, which can be more or less permanent and include relatively passive and/or active customers.

For engagement happiness, you need a certain type of co-creation, event marketing and social media—namely, co-creation with a stake, splashy events and the social media of the moment.

CO-CREATION WITH A STAKE

Co-creation is most engaging for customers when they feel that they have a stake in what the company does, or ideally, when customers create the product entirely on their own.

Based on this idea, customer participation in product design is the lowest co-creation touch that a company can offer. While it clearly transcends the traditional "active-company versus passive user" mentality, it may also come off simply as a source of cheap ideas. Nonetheless, customers, especially the fans of the brand, may feel somewhat appreciated and help the company. For example, crowd-sourcing techniques in B2B and B2C environments allow customers to make suggestions about the coffee and coffee environment they may want (see Starbucks), the T shirts they desire (threadless.com) or the grid technologies that may be used in the future (GE).

One step up is customization. Customization offers real value to the customer. Here, the user contributes to his or her product design and can immediately see the benefits. It has been used for mobile phone, print and TV apps.

Finally, open source is the ultimate engaged community with a stake, although the stake may not be financial. The open-source movement, since around the year 2000, is closely associated with the software revolution. However, there has also been an Open-Cola, for example. As Wikipedia reports, the original version 1.0 was released on January 27, 2001, and as of the writing of this book, the current version is 1.1.3. It was originally intended as a promotional tool to explain open source to the public, but the drink took on a life of its own and has sold some 150,000 cans. Check Wikipedia, itself an open source, for updates.[17]

Open source seems to work best for digital products (like Wikipedia with its millions of users and contributors) and much less well for physical goods (the 150,000 cans for OpenCola is dismal!). Let's look at a B2B example of how co-creation is being used in the emerging field of mobile money.

Moving Mobile Money into Afghanistan

As the term implies, mobile money gives users the ability to perform a variety of financial services via their mobile phones. A few examples are interfacing with one's bank account, mobile banking, transferring money for retail or other payments and mobile payments. The industry is still in its infancy, with players from Telcos and credit card companies to handset makers, app developers and banks trying to figure out which of the many delivery methods will ultimately be the most widely adopted by users. If they can reach a tipping point of widespread adoption, all will be happy players, and some companies will be at the center of a multibillion-dollar industry. Success, however, requires co-creation in which everybody has a stake.

They all strive for the best, most efficient, most secure, most convenient use of this emerging technology. Consider the potential scale of mobile money: globally, there are about 5 billion mobile phone users. Out of that number, a full one billion are "un-banked," meaning they don't have access to commercial financial services such as a bank account.

Mobile money technology is already being used in a growing number of scattered deployments around the world, both developed and emerging. There is still huge potential for growth, especially in the developing world. It's estimated that the global market for mobile payments will reach more than USD 600 billion by 2013.[18]

For places like London or Hong Kong, the mobile money adoption challenge is fairly easy. The environment is already technology-rich and full of ready users, and the impact is more one of convenience. But go to Haiti, Somalia or Afghanistan and the need for, and challenges of, setting up such a system are varied and complex. There could also be a more significant impact there—in the case of migrant workers, for example, sending money home in a matter of keystrokes.

The Central Asia Development Group (CADG) works in nineteen of the thirty-four provinces in Afghanistan. It is an established program implementer of third-party funds (such as the United States Agency for International Development, or USAID, and the Canadian International Development Agency, or CIDA) and reaches out to communities to plan and manage infrastructure projects ranging from road repair to canal cleaning to the building of dams and retaining walls for flood control. The projects have already employed almost 145,000 Afghan men and women who have few other opportunities for meaningful work.

CADG is piloting mobile money technology in Afghanistan. They are challenging themselves with an eventual goal of having some 200,000 Afghan employees connected, so that they can safely, easily and transparently receive their monthly salary.

With mobile money, such payments can be sent directly to an individual's mobile wallet, which is like your leather wallet, only it holds e-money instead of cash.

Once received, many things can be done with the e-money, including sending cash to family or purchasing airtime directly from the phone. The user can also exchange his or her e-money for hard currency from a nearby trusted mobile money agent.

And it's secure. If someone loses their leather wallet, for example, the cash usually vanishes. If a person loses their mobile phone, no one can access the e-money without a secret PIN. Even better, the system they are using in Afghanistan is accessible to all regardless of language or literacy and can be operated by voice instead of written menus in the Dari, Pashto and English languages.

By working together with local partners in Afghanistan, CADG is supporting the growth of the local mobile money eco-system that offers alternative access to financial services in a highly volatile, highly illiterate and often corrupt country.

It will take co-creation, collaboration and time to implement the scheme in Afghanistan, as everywhere else. But when CADG gets the right formula, it could be used as a model in other countries where man-made or natural disasters hinder money transfer.

SPLASH EVENTS

Effective happiness-creating events include direct, highly interactive and local consumer-brand encounters. They frequently occur face to face. They can result in a powerful temporary community that fully immerses the customer in the experience.

Companies use a variety of event formats. These differ in their potential for "splashiness."[19] Mass-sponsored events, for example, are events in which companies associate the brand with sports, music or arts events and stage various activities that relate the brand to the event. The Olympic Games, for example, is a sought-after global event. More than 50 corporate sponsors have already signed up for the 2012 London games, including several big global brands. The Beijing 2008 Olympic Games attracted household names such as Coca-Cola, Johnson & Johnson, and McDonald's and Chinese brands like Lenovo and Bank of China. All wanted to associate themselves with the spirit of the Olympic Games.

Coca-Cola, a sponsor of the Olympic Games since 1928, went beyond the usual logo blasting, trying to engage customers more directly, and spreading the sentiment of happiness that is part of its core values (see chapter 5) and the essence of its Chinese name translation (the Chinese characters used for Coca-Cola mean "Delicious Happiness"). The company distributed special commemorative cans and bottles to mark its presence at the games. Moreover, Coca-Cola provided refreshment for many thousands of athletes, families and fans who participated in the event; it also staged a "sports experience" station where fans could interact with athletes and take photos with them and presented the "Live Positively Award" at a special ceremony.

Trade shows, where companies present their brands to both clients and consumers, can be splash events as well. They offer consumers the opportunity to examine, interact with and test the brand. This type of event marketing is common in the automotive, consumer electronics, food, furniture and design sectors. For example, the annual auto shows held at attractive locations in major cities attract millions of consumers worldwide. To catch viewers' attention, car companies often employ leggy models and stage spectacular shows using video, sound and lighting effects. There are also numerous interactive activities and opportunities to participate in contests, product trials and celebrity guest appearances.

In addition to sponsored events and trade shows, companies are increasingly investing in more unconventional events such as street events. They are viewed as a form of guerrilla marketing and are organized on a local basis. Vodafone, BMW, Burger King, Avon and others have organized such street-marketing events. This type of event permits direct contact between the brand and consumers, facilitating a face-to-face interaction with brand performers and actors. For example, in the UK, Vodafone brought a cricket competition to a street event, complete with DJ music, barbecues, drinks and special appearances by legends of the game. These may be smaller events, to be sure, but they can be quite engaging and receive a lot of PR. Let's take a look at how energy-drink maker Red Bull has engaged customers in this way.

Red Bull Events: "It Gives You Wings"

The Austrian brand Red Bull, an energy drink, is masterful at supporting a wide variety of sports. On the professional sporting side, the ubiquitous logo shows up on everything from racing cars to motocross motorcycles, sailboats and stunt planes.

In addition to participating as a sponsor of Formula One, NASCAR and Extreme Sailing, since 1991 the logo has also been all over smaller events like Flugtag, an event in which amateurs build an airplane from everyday materials and then try to fly across a lake. In keeping with the company tag line, "It gives you wings," in 2000, the farthest flight at Red Bull Flugtag Austria went 195 feet. A new US record was set in 2007 when a flying banjo soared 155 feet! Aside from making great TV, the event is fun, but it has a serious amateur competitive side to it as well.

Through its website, Facebook, Twitter and mobile apps, Red Bull attracts customers and then holds interesting events to keep them engaged. Consider its nationwide scavenger hunts and procrastination games. During one hunt called the Red Bull Stash, the company hid its new Energy Shots all around the US and then posted Facebook clues as to where they could be found. It also hosts soapbox car racing and even does something called "Drunkish Dials" recordings. With this, Red Bull customers call a company toll-free hotline and leave "drunkish" messages which are then put on the Red Bull website. Funny and very edgy! Such a strategy makes sense because they target a young audience that appreciates this kind of engagement.

In fact, in addition to events, Red Bull engages its customers mostly through social media. Just about every time an article talks about the top companies in social media, Red Bull is at or near the top of those lists. Mashable, an online social-media news site, calls the company one of the "5 Most Engaged Brands in Social Media."[20]

THE SOCIAL MEDIA OF THE MOMENT

Social media are *the* new marketing tool for marketers. Red Bull may be ahead of the curve, but every company uses social media, even though many don't know the why or how quite yet. That's okay; because social media are so new, we must experiment. Will customers, however, at some point fall out of love with social media? Is it a fad, or will it soon become an established business practice like quality management, branding, or having a website?

I think it is quickly becoming the latter. Within a very short time span, social media have become a "must-have" instrument. The types of social media that are in vogue will change. But as easy, cheap global connectivity has finally arrived among customers on this planet, they are not giving up on it. People are, after all, social animals. There is no turning back.

Social media are essential for customer engagement and for sharing happiness.[21] They not only link individual customers; they also create entire customer networks. And they change all the time. So you don't want to be left behind. That's why it is important to always use the latest medium in each application. In sum, you need the social media of the moment.

Chorus

Let's consider one social media start up that can help you understand what customers think and feel. Chorus is an Australian B2B company, still in beta as of this writing. This new technology is a real-time, analytical, online text-mining tool that analyzes messages from your customers in real time, allowing you to accurately monitor what and how customers are feeling "right now."[22] Chorus and other similar services are great tools for planning your happiness campaigns.

Chorus looks at everything customers say, whether via e-mail, social networking or elsewhere in cyberspace. Through an algorithmic solution, it posts real-time updates about customer feelings regarding certain products, even your competition's. By using this tool, you can increase customer loyalty by finding out (and providing) what your customers consider great customer service and what will surprise them. This can also lead to targeted marketing campaigns.[23]

Consider the case of an equipment rental supplier. The company experienced customer unhappiness and wanted to increase customer satisfaction.[24] They had already streamlined workflows and received reports on key metrics like average handle time, but had not figured out what exactly was most irritating to current, new and prospective customers. By analyzing e-mails, tweets and blog posts, Chorus detected that complex forms and hidden charges were the main reasons for customer angst.

Moreover, Chorus was able to monitor all inbound e-mails to the company and immediately detected a number of customers currently suffering from a natural disaster. A marketing campaign quickly identified these customers for a special promotion offering assistance, which delighted them.

By monitoring all inbound customer-support e-mails, the rental company was able to understand exactly what was frustrating its customers and fix the problems they discovered. This clearly shows that harnessing information from various social media can be very useful in engaging and pleasing customers.

CONCLUSION

In this chapter, we identified the key touchpoints for pleasure, meaning and engagement happiness. As I said at the beginning, if pleasure happiness is your goal, think like a designer and put together a design- and aesthetics-focused team, a retail team that focuses on experience and a service team that focuses on service surprises and customer delight. You also need to instill that sort of mentality in your retail-channel and service partners.

If meaning happiness is your goal, you need to think like an anthropologist and be in close touch with values that are prevalent in a community or culture. To do so, your product team must focus on the essence of the product and brand more than on its aesthetics. You need a communication agency that strives for authenticity and a CSR campaign on a mission.

Finally, for engagement happiness, you need to think like a production team and engage in co-creation, where customers have a stake, stage splash events and consider the social media of the moment.

Most importantly, you need to communicate to everyone that customer happiness is the key objective. Your designers, your retail, service, communication, event and social-media agencies and partners (internally and externally)—all must focus on customer happiness. That requires you to use approaches at these touchpoints that target specific kinds of customer happiness and express the insights gained about your customers. You do not want a generic design and retail approach with the usual service maps, communication and events.

How to put your organization on a happiness footing is the topic of the next chapter.

7

HOW TO GET YOUR ORGANIZATION FOCUSED ON CUSTOMER HAPPINESS

In the previous chapters we used insights from positive psychology to discuss methods for making customers happy by providing them with products and services that can instill pleasure, meaning and engagement. Additionally, we discussed several examples of successful implementations at various touchpoints.

What resources and skills are required from your organization to deliver happiness? How do you put your organization on a happiness footing? Do you need to get the organization to focus on certain tasks?

In this chapter, I will present the core organizational requirements to deliver customer happiness on a sustainable basis. I will present a five-step framework that any organization can use to move along the customer happiness journey and deliver happiness in more consistent ways. As you know, the end point of this journey is to view happiness as a business goal. To get there, we need to: (1) adopt the customer's perspective; (2) gain customer insight; (3) use left brain and right brain thinking to generate creative ideas about customers; (4) incorporate customer input in customer-relevant decision making; and (5) create a customer-focused culture. Let's look at each step and some examples.

STEP 1: ADOPT THE CUSTOMER'S PERSPECTIVE

The journey begins with taking the perspective of the customer, seeing the world through their eyes or standing in their shoes.

Psychologists tell us that adopting the perspective of others, customers or not, requires empathy—the ability to experience the thoughts and feelings of other people as if they were our own. It is an ability that must be learned. Young children show empathy in very rudimentary ways. Affective empathy develops only between the ages of eight to twelve. So-called metacognition develops even later. Some individuals—those with a condition called narcissistic personality disorder—never get good at it. They are largely unable and unwilling to identify and acknowledge the thoughts and feelings of others.

Adopting the customer's perspective is equally hard for organizations. The reason is often corporate narcissism. Like Narcissus, who in Greek mythology fell in love with his own reflection, many corporations, especially those that are engineering-driven, are in love with their own products and technologies. They refuse to acknowledge that consumers may desire different features or other service elements or may have simply fallen out of love with what the company has to offer.

But this lack of customer perspective extends beyond engineering-driven organizations. Creative agencies, for example, can display the same narcissistic bias. They may fail to understand that customers care less about design, coolness or looks than the agency does. They often don't appreciate that their customers' happiness may be driven by values other than hedonism.

When you are serious about customer happiness, make sure to adopt the customer's point of view as often as possible. This first step in the organizational journey does not require extensive investment, just some perspective-taking and sharpening of your observational skills. Surround yourself with the product or service, and then assume the attitude of a naïve user.

For example, if you design signage for airports or public transportation systems, walk around like a user. Pretend to be someone who is not familiar with the signs and their symbols and language; search for the exit, a restroom, a gate or track. Choose targets that are not easy to find. Observe where the arrows point. Experience the frustration and unhappiness that a user may experience if he or she is suddenly lost. You must make the signage foolproof from a user's point of view.

Observing customers and seeing the world through their eyes is particularly useful in identifying obstacles toward customer happiness. Here is an example of a fabulous new invention that has the potential to improve the lives of many people around the world and help them live happier lives. It is a product that was not developed with a lot of customer research, but simply by empathizing with and observing users.

THE LEVERAGED FREEDOM CHAIR

The Leveraged Freedom Chair (LFC) is a new wheelchair developed for disabled people in developing markets. It is not on the market yet, but it has been tested in India and has already won design awards.

Having worked for a couple of years in my early twenties with paraplegics at a rehabilitation center in Germany, I am well aware of how small changes in the maneuverability of a wheelchair can make a world of difference for somebody who is physically impaired. I used a wheelchair several times in order to see what it felt like. The experience can be quite frustrating, even with some of the most advanced and expensive products. Yet when a wheelchair can be easily maneuvered, it becomes a sort of second body and can significantly add to a person's life satisfaction.

Now, imagine what a difference the right wheelchair can make if you are physically impaired and living in the countryside, especially in a place like rural India. Modern electric wheelchairs do not work well on the rough terrain and unpaved roads that crisscross towns and connect villages. Limited or close-to-no mobility means limited access to opportunities and a significantly diminished quality of life. People may not have access to work or a trip to the store or market, or they may simply not be able to enjoy time with family or friends.

The LFC designed at the Massachusetts Institute of Technology (MIT) Mobility Lab provides a solution that will tremendously help disabled people in rural areas. The wheelchair was created by Dr. Amos Winter, a postdoctoral researcher who will soon be an MIT professor, and Dr. Dan Frey, an MIT professor and mechanical engineer whose research and work focus on the design of engineering systems. Robust design ensures that engineering systems function despite variations in manufacturing, wear, deterioration and environmental conditions. Winter was the leader of the design team, and Frey was the faculty advisor to the team.

The LFC is maneuverable within the home and can travel long distances on rough roads. "The Leverage Freedom Chair uses the chain-and-sprocket drive train of a standard bicycle in conjunction with two extended push levers," Frey explained to me when I visited him. I couldn't entirely follow his design explanations, but the levers on the chair provide a change in mechanical advantage. The user simply slides his or her hands upward on the lever to increase the torque applied. This gives the user a four-to-one change in mechanical advantage. The overrunning clutch, the so-called freewheel, from a bicycle is also essential as it allows the lever to be drawn backward to start a new power stroke.

This is a huge advantage on bad terrain. To operate the wheelchair, the user can push forward on the levers to propel the chair forward. To go through mud, the user grabs high on the lever to maximize leverage. To go fast, the user changes gears by grabbing and pushing low on the levers. This ingenious system gives a disabled individual access to the roughest terrain while allowing more speed on smoother terrain than in a normal wheelchair. The wheelchair can also be used indoors by simply removing the levers.

"But the advantage is not only greater maneuverability," Frey told me. "It also works different and more desirable muscle groups and may thus have health effects as well." The wheelchair has a targeted cost of about USD 200, far less than most commercial options. "It may even become an attractive lifestyle option as a second wheelchair for users in developed countries."

Being in the rural villages with the users and observing them was an essential part of the design process. Winter told me that some of the key design refinements came from careful observation. "For example, people with difficulty controlling their upper body position were having trouble with one of the early prototypes," he said. "When they pushed on the levers, they did not have adequate support for the needed reaction force. A change in seat configuration that made the backrest taller greatly improved the ergonomics of the chair." Other refinements, such as ways to remove and store the levers and ways to implement the brakes, were also strongly tied to customer observation and feedback.

STEP 2: GAIN IN-DEPTH CUSTOMER INSIGHT

Customer insight is gleaned from all sorts of information collection techniques, from traditional market research (including surveys and focus groups) to ethnographic techniques (such as spending time with customers) to new non-conscious, psychophysiological techniques (like brain scanning, eye-movement tracking and galvanic skin response). The measures can be quantitative or qualitative. They can be one-shot data collection or longitudinal studies that may result in millions of observations or five to ten deep dives.

The variety and sophistication of these measures is mindboggling. Moreover, tools are constantly expanding. Data mining is no longer just mining of numbers. As consumers are increasing their conversations online, marketers have started to listen in and to use text-mining techniques to plot these conversations and the feelings that arise from them. In the future, as customers express their views about products and brands not through ratings and words, but primarily by posting images and video, movable visual-image mining may be the next frontier. Imagine the data and computing requirements for that!

Using these tools is important for gaining customer insight from every angle. But this does not necessarily mean that all of these techniques must be used simultaneously. Keep things in perspective and focus on the essentials. Do not get carried away by new technologies. Some of them may be sexy from a technological or scientific point of view, but their value for business may be questionable. That is, they may be great tools for scientific insight but fall short as practical tools for customer insight. They may satisfy the needs of the researcher but may not be useful for gaining insight about the customer.

When you are trying to gain consumer insight, you must get close to consumers to understand how they live and how your product can improve their lives. Likewise, when you conduct insight studies in B2B settings, you must understand business customers' processes and how your solution can add value to them. So, whether you are in B2C or B2B businesses, it is important not to lose track of your target and the insight that you are trying to achieve. Let me illustrate my point with a consumer example that involves, once again, India and MIT.

P&G'S LOCAL INSIGHTS

In 2002, Gillette decided to enter the fast-growing Indian market with a razor designed specifically for low-income Indian men. Unlike Western men, most Indian men shave only a couple of times a week. When Gillette developed its razor for the Indian market, it tested it on Indian men. Being based in Boston, it decided to recruit Indian students from MIT. The students loved the new product, but it did not do particularly well when introduced into the Indian market. What Gillette had forgotten was that the MIT students, unlike many men in India, had access to running water. The students were able to rinse the razor easily. But in rural India, water is often sparse, and shaving is viewed as a social experience that takes place at a barber shop. Eight years later, in October 2010, Gillette, which was bought by P&G in 2005, introduced another razor, the Gillette Guard, with a blade that was easy to rinse and clean and was cheap. It was marketed with local appeal including Indian dancing in a village community. The successful new razor was developed based on the consumer insight philosophy at P&G: develop products for local markets and get close to consumers.

"We seek deep knowledge and insight into where people and markets are and where they're going," Joan M. Lewis, P&G's Global Consumer and Market Knowledge Officer, explained to me. "We go beyond consumer understanding to discover the 'not yet obvious' motivations and tensions that inspire ideas and actions. We study what people do, how they behave and the choices they make. And we personally interact with people in the places they live and work. We place people at the heart of our corporate and brand strategies."

This consumer insight philosophy is part of CEO Robert McDonald's "purpose-inspired growth strategy" of "touching and improving more lives, in more parts of the world, more completely." McDonald has set an ambitious goal of reaching 5 billion consumers by 2015; at the time of this writing, P&G has already reached 4.4 billion. The company is shifting its focus from the US and other Western markets to emerging markets in Asia and Africa.

Much of this growth is coming from what we called in chapter 2, following C. K. Prahalad, "the bottom of the pyramid"— meaning the very poor.[1] P&G is not the only company that is targeting such consumers. When I attended a customer insight conference in New Delhi in the summer of 2011, the bottom of the pyramid was the major topic explored. As a result of vast disparities in incomes (some are quite rich but three quarters of the population make less than USD 2 per day) and living conditions (rural areas or crowded urban markets), consumers at the bottom of the hierarchy in the developing world are very different from consumers at the medium or top of the pyramid in the developed world. They may prefer different razors, shampoo, cleaning or skin care products and may respond differently to marketing communications. That's why P&G feels that local consumer insight is required.

Many of the insight tools are ethnographic in nature. Applying observational learning methods, using skills from ethnography and anthropology, modern-day ethnographic consumer researchers spend time with rural Indian and Chinese consumers to gain their trust and observe their daily practices in order to understand their living conditions and habits.

The researcher is hoping to find the pearl of consumer insight that can be translated into a successful product that adds value to the consumer and can therefore improve lives.

How does it work in practice? For example, a researcher and scientist from Cincinnati, P&G's headquarters, together with a photographer and a translator, may observe a rural consumer in a Chinese province wash her hair with a liquid shampoo. She may use a small basin with only three cups of rainwater because water is precious and expensive. She may only do a cursory rinse and then use the family comb to comb through her tangles. In her day-to-day washing, she usually uses laundry soap flakes that make her hair oily.[2] But she notes that she loves her long hair, its shininess, and feels happy after taking care of it.

The methodology can also be applied to the top-of-the-pyramid segment—for example, by observing the daily skin-care routines of newly wealthy, lifestyle-conscious Chinese consumers.

"This deep consumer understanding allows us to create and deliver products that are as common as possible to enable scale, and as different as needed, to activate locally," said Lewis. "This way, we can better serve consumers as they want to be served."

Gaining in-depth insight is important. But how exactly do you get from initial observations to sparking a new idea? That's what we'll explore in our next step.

STEP 3: MAKE USE OF LEFT BRAIN/RIGHT BRAIN

Call it analytical versus intuitive, or detail-oriented versus holistic. Or the classic left brain/right brain. These are the terms commonly used to understand different thinking and working styles.

When an organization wants to think about its customers creatively and innovatively, it needs staff that can think about customers from multiple angles. Ideally, they should be able to think both analytically and outside the box. For many business people, analytical thinking is more natural; unconventional thinking is often a challenge.

Therefore, you need to cobble together diverse work teams that include individuals with different skills and thinking styles—both analytical and outside-the-box thinkers. Creativity is defined as the ability to conjure something new and useful. It cannot consist of just free-wheeling *divergent* thinking (thinking outside the box); it also requires *convergent* thinking (bringing it all back into a new box).

In a recent project for the American Association of Nurse Anesthetists, I conducted a creative exercise in which I asked the participating nurses to use Starbucks as a benchmark for improving the operating room experience. The nurses came up with all sorts of ideas for raising a patient's happiness while being sedated: using an aromatherapy mask, playing cool music or serving a cup of coffee before being knocked out. Subsequently, they evaluated the feasibility of these ideas. The results showed that some were great, while others not as good. In sum, as part of the creative process, you also need a thorough evaluation phase.

IDEO is a prominent design and innovation consulting firm based in California. The firm helps companies generate and implement creative ideas. Here is an example from a hospital-room project. The challenge: improve the hospital-room experience so that patients feel less unhappy.

Paul Bennett told me how IDEO approached the project. I first met him when he was just "Paul," and part of a small creative boutique agency in New York City called "Nick and Paul." That was more than ten years ago. Nick and Paul (the people and the firm) showed up as guest speakers in my MBA class, and what a class it was! The two were dressed in rough leather jackets and related story after story of provoking and shaking up their corporate clients' established beliefs. Most of my students—typically analytic-minded spreadsheet users—were not familiar with the firm. Nor did they know how to react; after the presentation, they wondered aloud who might really hire these guys. When I met Paul again ten years later, in the summer of 2011, he still seemed a bit of a rebel at heart. He stands apart from the corporate crowd, in his looks (the way he dresses and expresses himself) and the way he speaks, using design lingo rather than corporate jargon. However, he is now the chief creative officer of IDEO. And people who know IDEO expect that sort of look and talk from a design firm. In other words, like Apple Computers and W Hotels, he's gone mainstream (no insult intended, Paul!).

Back to the project. When asked to explain what constitutes the "hospital-room experience," the firm told the client, "Just look up!" One of the IDEO designers had checked into a hospital room and filmed the experience of lying there flat on the bed. IDEO then showed a 10-minute video of the ceiling to the client, with the face of a doctor or nurse occasionally popping into the picture. The point: staring at the ceiling *is* the hospital-room experience. Out of this came a simple and brilliant idea: use the ceiling as a canvas for showing useful information or soothing images. I'd certainly be happier in that hospital.

No left-brain, analytical, detail-oriented thinking or data crunching alone would have gotten you to this idea. To generate a creative idea, you need right-brain, intuitive, holistic thinking. When it comes to implementation, though, you need to check the details. You need to include the hospital specialists, facilities managers, perhaps even the doctors (with their traditionally left-brain thinking), to ensure that the information and images placed on the ceiling will not cause a heart attack, seizure or other physical malady.[3]

STEP 4: CONSIDER CUSTOMER INPUT IN ALL DECISIONS

After you have adopted the customer's perspective, gained in-depth customer insight and used your right and left brain to come up with creative ideas for customers, it's time to make use of that customer input you gathered earlier. Seems obvious, right?

No, it is not. In many organizations, lots of detailed customer information is collected over time; at any given moment, some of it may be relevant and the rest may be dated. But shortage of data is usually not the problem. The problem is that the collected data are often not used at all. They are not used to make decisions on new products, on how to provide good service to customers, on how to treat loyal customers or on anything else.

This is because market researchers, customer-insight specialists and creative staff are not always taken seriously by senior decision makers within an organization, such as regional managing directors, the chief marketing officer or other senior management. In fact, market researchers and insight specialists often view themselves as number-crunching support staff whose only purpose is to liaise with a marketing research firm to commission quarterly data. Worse, some are academics in disguise; they just love to play with datasets and don't worry much about their relevance to business and customers.

This needs to change. Customer input and customer intelligence must be considered for a variety of decisions. To this end, the Boston Consulting Group's (BCG) Consumer Insight Group issued a 2009 benchmarking report that presents a four-stage model based on a survey of insight functions in 40 global corporations, all industry leaders.[4]

At Stage 1, customer input is considered part of the traditional marketing function and rarely has any impact outside marketing. At Stage 2, customer input contributes to specific business decisions. At Stage 3, it is used for important strategy decisions (though mostly to justify them retroactively). At Stage

4, customer input is used for strategic foresight. Clearly, the best place for your customer insight group to be is at Stage 4.

STEP 5: CREATE A CUSTOMER HAPPINESS–FOCUSED CULTURE

Finally, Step 5 constitutes a transformative stage. As the organization uses the various input collected from the wide variety of decisions, it transforms itself into a customer-focused organization. And this customer-focused organization should focus on customer happiness. That is, it must define, as a key corporate objective, the creation of positive emotions and feelings among customers. This should be done by focusing on daily pleasures, meaning creation and ongoing engagement. In other words, everybody's job in the organization is to contribute, in whatever they do, to customer happiness.

With Step 5, we have reached the ultimate goal: the company makes customer happiness its business focus.

Remember the quote by John Mackey, founder and CEO of Whole Foods Market, from the end of chapter 1: "In the customer-centered business, customer happiness is an end in itself, and will be pursued with greater interest, passion, and empathy than the profit-centered business is capable of." Remember that Starwood's Barry Sternlicht developed the new W chain because he felt the market needed a happier place for cool travelers. Remember that UNIQLO's founder wanted to empower people by allowing them to create a unique style at an affordable price. Remember that Yuhan-Kimberly wanted to keep Korea green. In the next chapter, we will describe HR policies at the Walt Disney World Resort in Florida. The emphasis, company officials there say, is not on profit, but on keeping the customer central to everything they do. These are companies that perfectly illustrate the spirit of happiness as a business focus.

Senior management must serve as role models for the rest of the organization of what it means to be an advocate for the interests of customers. I'd like to close this chapter with a detailed case study of a large organization that, through the leadership of senior management, has transformed itself from a culture focused purely on engineering and efficiency toward becoming a customer-happiness culture: Samsung Electronics.

THE SAMSUNG TRANSFORMATION[5]

In October 2009, Samsung Electronics invited me to give a talk on how they could become a "love brand." This struck me as a strange assignment. Images of Woodstock and "free love" popped into my head. Did Samsung want to embrace a hippie culture? I remembered the cultural roots of the company and its electronics business in South Korea in the 1960s. I concluded that Samsung is not, and never could be, a "love brand" in the sense that Apple is. I tried to communicate this message politely to my audience of marketers and engineers. It was clear to me that it would be impossible to transform Samsung from a technology-driven firm that relied on its solid engineering know-how to a customer-oriented organization that used technology to appeal to lifestyle and emotions.

At the end of my talk, as if to prove me wrong, an employee from Samsung Digital Imaging proudly handed me a slim box. Inside was Samsung's newest digital camera, which had launched in September 2009, the 2View camera. (It is called the DualView camera in the US, for copyright reasons.) "Here," he said, "give this a try and see what you think."

The 2View camera represented two years of research, planning and design, and was a headliner in the company's effort to rebrand itself as a creative, risk-taking consumer-electronics maker. It was developed with customer insight input from Samsung's Product Innovation Team located in California.

The primary feature of the 2View is its two LCD screens—the traditional one on the back of the camera, and a second one on the front. As I used the camera, I began to understand that the front screen serves multiple uses that are also very enjoyable: it helps individuals take better self-portraits (they can see the image as they take the picture); it displays a countdown ("3, 2, 1 . . .") for use during timed photos and it has a "child" function that plays short animated movies to keep toddlers looking (and smiling) at the camera while being photographed. Samsung hoped this front-screen feature would move it into the top ranks of digital-camera makers, allowing it to challenge or even surpass its longtime Japanese digital camera rivals like Canon and Sony. After all, by the late 2000s, Samsung had become number one or two in many digital categories: LCD televisions, high-memory chips, smartphones and other products. But it lagged behind in digital cameras.

Digital Imaging had previously been part of Samsung's precision machinery affiliate (called Samsung Techwin), where it developed imaging components such as lenses and camera viewfinders as well as surveillance products. Being part of Samsung Techwin, the division was also making consumer cameras, but most were low-priced commodity items, selling for under USD 150 and released mainly with the intention of offering decent technology at a cost slightly below the competition. Techwin's engineers and sales force did not consider its customers to be ordinary people capturing their precious memories on camera but, instead, saw their consumers as the retail distributors, mainly discount stores, looking for non-premium brands. In fact, until recently, that has been their business model not just for cameras but also for many other electronic products.

"I had to change the mindset of my people," Sang-Jin Park, CEO of Samsung Digital Imaging, told me when I first met him. "They didn't pay any attention to the consumers and how they used a camera to take pictures."

Having turned around other parts of its electronics business by focusing on consumers, Samsung wanted to bring that same kind of end-user, consumer-oriented focus to its imaging business. This required permanently changing the mindset of Samsung Digital Imaging's R&D and their marketing teams from one based on purely technical, mechanical and price considerations to one based on consumer lifestyle, experience and emotions. Because the efforts were all about exploring and defining new ground, Park named his initiative "Project Columbus."[6]

Park first noted that product quality had suffered since cameras hadn't been a high priority for Samsung. One day he showed up on the factory floor and marched over to the area where cameras that didn't meet the company's standards during the quality-assurance process were stockpiled. He took the box of rejects and dumped them on the floor in the center of the factory—and set fire to them as employees looked on. The message was clear: low standards wouldn't be tolerated.

But the problems weren't limited to quality. Samsung did not develop new and exciting products that consumers loved and that made them happy. Park ordered a full-scale market research effort to find out what consumers really needed and wanted. He focused on three key elements: design, innovation and consumer experience. He then turned to Samsung's new laboratory for customer insight and customer-driven innovation, the Product Innovation Team (PIT), in the heart of California's Silicon Valley.

A few weeks later, in January 2010, I visited PIT in San Jose. PIT served an agency-like function, supporting various Samsung businesses in their quest to make their product development processes more customer-centric. PIT's mission was to spread a new product quality definition within Samsung: that product quality is no longer measured purely by engineering or manufacturing conformity but also by whether the product provides the right experience to customers.

Walking into the PIT offices felt like stepping into a small Googleplex (as Google's nearby headquarters are called). The walls were painted with bright primary colors, a pool table stood in one corner and surfaces were piled with magazines—not just technology publications, but fashion, lifestyle and car magazines. The objective, clearly, was for employees not just to work, but to relax and play as well. There were movable walls, whiteboards filled with doodles and notes and a private room where workers could nap, breast-feed or meditate. All the employees, including the director, Yoon Lee, dressed casually.

Lee, a Korean American with a passion for vintage sports cars, was trained in engineering and manufacturing and worked as a consultant at Accenture before spearheading the development of Samsung's innovation lab in 2006. The organization was lean: he had eight employees by early 2010—including a former venture capitalist, an ex-Palm product manager and a consumer insight researcher. He said that all the team members were passionate about consumer electronics and were therefore intrinsically motivated. "For them, this isn't work. This is an extension of their lives." He added, "The Korean Americans among us are proud to see an innovative Samsung now. This is exciting for us." By now, PIT has launched similar labs in other locations around the world, including London, Shanghai and Singapore.

When PIT opened, it was given one task: develop customer insight–driven product concepts that would position Samsung as a cutting-edge, market-driven global brand. Among its first prototypes was a massive vending machine co-branded with Coca-Cola; it debuted at the Beijing Olympics, where it made a big splash. Rather than just showing the drinks, the machine had an interactive LCD touch screen that could also play short films and advertisements and show animated logos for the available products. It had some other impressive capabilities, too; for example, if a child came up to the machine, it detected the customer's size and the display shifted downward, to a child's eye level. Samsung called its creation not a vending machine but a "brand media kiosk."

PIT employees spent their days coming up with these kinds of ideas and concepts. For easy testing, they had a 3-D printer in the back room, along with a machine that quickly and automatically builds prototypes out of various materials. This allowed them to come up with ideas, print mock-ups of products and discuss them within minutes.

PIT's greatest success so far was the 2View camera. Through surveys and segmentation studies, they found a few possible directions, mainly concerning how to make cameras to better support the new imaging lifestyle. The researchers also discerned a subtle theme in their interviews and surveys: consumers were taking more and more photos of themselves. They were snapping self-portraits for their Facebook pages and their online-dating profiles and recording their every move for their blogs and personal websites. These suggested a self-expressive undercurrent in consumer behavior, a desire to constantly document and share one's life with a vast network of friends and strangers.

PIT seized on this insight, and out of it came the 2View Camera. Although the 2View incorporated several useful features like the countdown and the child function, its primary attraction was the ease with which users could now shoot self-portraits and photos of themselves with friends. There was nothing like it on the shelves. So Samsung decided to charge a premium price (USD 349 and USD 299 for its two models in the US).

The target segment for the camera would be what Samsung called the "Style Prestige" segment—married, professional women from ages 25 to 34, who would appreciate both the camera's functions and its sleek black-and-red design. Samsung's expectation was that their target consumers would enjoy owning a camera with a stylish design and taking successful self-portraits with it; therefore, they would be willing to pay a premium price.

When the PIT team brought the 2View idea to Samsung's engineers, the engineers initially objected for technical reasons. No supplier was manufacturing the tiny screens necessary for 2View's front screen. They also argued that the resolution would be different between the two screens, making it impossible for users to turn both front and back screens at the same time to display the images at their natural resolution. Finally, the engineers felt the 2View didn't showcase their own unique skills enough. After all, they said, LCD screens were not a new technology and screens were getting bigger and bigger, not smaller. Ultimately, however, the engineers embraced these constraints as a technical challenge and got excited about developing the product.

To prepare the trade for the launch, Samsung first cleared out its old inventory. Then Sang-Jin Park activated the global sales force and impressed upon the salespeople that they were to sell not just the technical features but the experience and excitement of using the camera. To that end, Park placed oversized cameras in stores, allowing shoppers to test the new functions, pose for the camera and play, all in keeping with the "fun" image Samsung wanted to project.

Samsung's Global Marketing Operations, jointly with Samsung Digital Imaging, developed the communications strategy for the 2View brand and hired advertising agency Leo Burnett to execute a consumer-focused ad campaign. The campaign emphasized not only the camera's features but the brand's intangible significance to consumers: imagination, optimism, style and fun. The essence of the creative idea was that the camera transformed how people took photos, making them into happy customers.

A TV ad showed cool, 30-ish people in a café in Europe taking a group photo using the front screen of the 2View camera. One of the young women in the group then takes a photo with a Beefeater guard, who breaks out of character and starts a parade of fun that ends up in a zoo where he takes a picture of a baby (using the "child" mode). A gorilla ultimately seizes the camera to take its own photo. Riffing off the double screens, the ad closed with the 2View's catchy tagline: "Twice the fun."

Prior to the August 2009 launch, Samsung Digital Imaging's marketing team created buzz through a coordinated new media campaign on Facebook, Twitter and YouTube. The company also began sending out samples to key technology writers, business analysts, and photography magazines. By the time the 2View arrived in stores in mid-September 2009, Samsung had collected positive comments from around the world, including a *New York Times* review by tech reviewer David Pogue calling the camera's two screens "a fresh (and genuinely useful) idea," and one in *USA Today* saying the camera was "straight of the 'Why didn't I think about that?' school of technology."

According to Samsung, the 2View's sales results surpassed projections. Samsung had initially planned to sell 500,000 cameras; in the first year, the actual shipment from September to December 2009 exceeded 800,000. The camera won 68 awards in 14 countries and was featured more than 6,000 times by major media outlets, with a public relations effect that Samsung valued at around USD 12 million.

The next time I met Sang-Jin Park was in Las Vegas at the January 2010 Consumer Electronics Show (CES), one of the most important trade gatherings for consumer electronics manufacturers. Here, all major manufacturers unveil their new products and dazzle retail executives and journalists with spectacular presentations and flashy displays, thus creating buzz for the coming year. Vegas, a city built on spectacle, is of course the perfect host for such a show.

At the Samsung booth, the company offered the usual presentations one finds at these events—a bunch of chairs set up in front of a screen and a person with a headset microphone running through the cameras' features. In short, it was neither captivating nor exciting.

The show-stopper was at the Casio booth, where dozens of techno-geeks crowded around a platform watching scantily clad women engaged in energetic martial-arts exercises, like board-breaking and sparring. What does this have to do with cameras?

Very little, except that Casio had placed several samples of its new model—the FH–100—along the stage area, snapped photos of the martial arts action, and then projected them onto big screens. Casio thus showed off, in an experiential way, the camera's various features, like the ability to shoot clear pictures of high-speed action. I could tell from watching the techno-geek's faces that many of them were very happy indeed.

Later that day, I met with Seung-Soo Park, the vice president for strategic marketing at Samsung Digital Imaging, and the first lieutenant to Sang-Jin Park. Over lunch, we discussed Digital Imaging's goal of transforming itself into a leader in innovative product development.

I asked him whether, despite the recent success of the 2View camera and other products, Samsung could still learn some lessons from some of its competitors—for example, how to showcase its products at a convention like the one here in Las Vegas. He immediately mentioned Apple. "From Apple we can certainly learn how to create buzz. But we also must look outside our industry for ideas. We could learn from Coke or even a cosmetics company," he said.

I also asked him for his impressions of the new Chinese firms at the trade show. "When I see them, I feel nostalgia," he said. "Just about ten years ago, we were like them. We had a small booth at CES, not in the main hall. We all went to the Japanese brands and said, 'Wow!' We went to our engineers and said, 'Help us make these kinds of products.' Now," he said, "it's the Chinese companies that are looking to copy and ultimately improve on Samsung's technology and design."

Samsung's recent success, in all sorts of electronic categories, has been undeniable. Yet would Samsung's skills and capabilities also serve it well in the future?

I asked this question in an interview of Sea-Jin Chang, a strategy professor and author of an important book on the rivalry between Sony and Samsung.[7] "Samsung didn't need a strategy before because they had someone to follow," Chang told me. "Now they're on the top, they have to defend that position. They have to figure out where technology is going, they have to understand consumers much better, and they have to make strategic decisions about what directions to take."

He continued, "Their strength is their ability to execute. They can develop a product fast, and they can get to market faster than others because of their speed of execution. To catch up, you can copy your competitors, but to sustain being a leader, you certainly need creativity and innovation."

Sang-Jin Park seemed well aware of the challenge to not only become customer-focused but to become, more broadly speaking, a creative culture. Over a dinner in a trendy wine bar and restaurant in Seoul, he told me that engineers and managers may have to give up their calcified notions of how Samsung operates in order to do things differently:

> *"I changed the whole process—putting consumers first, getting insight from consumer surveys to find out what were the unmet needs, and then bringing those ideas to R&D, and then to marketing, so we can communicate better with dealers and with consumers. Now we have to repeat that success."*

CONCLUSION

The case of Samsung and the 2View Camera illustrates the up-and-down struggle of trying to implement a customer happiness focus in a large organization. It is not enough to adopt the customer's perspective; you also need to verify and deepen it with customer insight. You need to generate creative ideas out of that insight and incorporate it into decisions that impact customers. And you need to make customer happiness your ultimate business focus.

The first step, adopting the customer perspective, is inexpensive. It requires a simple, but not necessarily easy, shift in thinking and observation. The second step requires investment in customer insight—specifically, setting up and funding an internal customer insight group. The third step involves creative thinking about customers, for which you need organizational teams that can bridge left-brain and right-brain thinking. Step 4 incorporates customer input in decision-making. Thus, in the organizational chart, your insight and creative people must be positioned near decision makers. Finally, Step 5 is about creating a customer happiness–focused culture, and that must be done from the very top down.

As we will see in the next chapter, a major part of creating a customer happiness–focused culture concerns *internal* customers—that is, employees. When they feel good, when they experience their work as meaningful, when they are engaged, they will go a long way toward making your external customers happy.

8

YOUR HAPPY WORKFORCE

Work is a pervasive and influential part of a person's life. The average adult spends a significant portion of his or her life working; estimates range from one third to one fourth. Moreover, work satisfaction contributes 20 to 25 percent to life satisfaction. One could argue that organizations have a moral responsibility to make their employees happy in the workplace.

Employee happiness also seems to be in the best interest of organizations. Happy employees will be more productive and interact more effectively with customers; this increases customer satisfaction. That's why companies have large human resources departments and spend significant amounts of money and resources on hiring the right employees, as well as training and developing them. Employee happiness is not just some sort of internal corporate social responsibility; in a very real sense, it can provide competitive advantage. That's why the *Harvard Business Review* published a special January/February 2012 issue entitled,

"The Value of Happiness: How Employee Well-Being Drives Profits."

In the years to come, employee happiness may become even more important because in many labor markets skilled labor will be in short supply. While technology has wiped some job categories off the map (think data entry or data manipulation), we still need workers and talent to service our growing population. In the US, for example, the shortage of skilled labor is already being felt in industries like manufacturing, utilities, energy, health care, and others that need skilled IT workers and researchers.[1] With the baby boomers now starting to retire, the much smaller Generation X and Generation Y won't have the people power to fill all the gaps. Thus, companies face additional costs for recruitment, development and retention. A survey by AC Nielsen found that more than two-thirds of responding companies expect the looming talent shortage to cost them at least USD 50 million. And one-third of those with revenues of more than USD 1 billion indicated that their costs would top USD 100 million. The US Bureau of Labor statistics already shows the disparity. In manufacturing, for example, the seasonally adjusted number of job openings swelled by 45 percent between October 2009 and October 2010. But the number of actual hires rose by only 11 percent.

In this chapter, we first discuss the long-standing hypothesis that "happy workers are productive workers." Is there any evidence for it? We then ask the question, "What makes employees happy?" It turns out there are numerous factors that affect employee happiness—from tangible benefits to social and personal factors to customization at work, authenticity and buzz, and the physical environment. On the way, we will hear about people management at Deloitte, Disney, a call center in Brazil and Frankfurt's New Work City.

POSITIVE ORGANIZATIONAL BEHAVIOR

In chapter 2, we discussed how the field of psychology had for 50 years been focused almost exclusively on the negative aspects of behavior. This negative perspective also characterized the fields of human resources (HR) and organizational behavior (OB). These fields, for example, paid a lot of attention to stress and burnout, resistance to change, dysfunctional managers and employees and deviant workplace behaviors; but they paid little attention to positive behaviors and outcomes at the workplace.

Only HR and OB gurus like Stephen Covey, author of the mega-bestseller *The Seven Habits of Highly Effective People*, addressed topics such as proactivity, empathy, positive teamwork and renewal.[2] His eldest son, Stephen M. R. Covey, contributed another essential positive concept: trust in organizations, which he believes dramatically speeds up decision making and organizational efficiency. Academic researchers, however, discounted these writings as unscientific.

Fred Luthans, an accomplished management professor and former president of the Academy of Management, changed that. What Martin Seligman did for the field of psychology, he did for the field of OB. Luthans, who teaches at the University of Nebraska, attended the first positive psychology conference in 1999 and left that gathering transformed:

> *"The papers presented at this and the subsequent academic conferences under the general leadership of internationally recognized research psychologists Martin Seligman and Ed Diener, provided a 'eureka' for me of how this positive approach could be taken to organizational behavior. This is what I had been searching for—a theory and research-driven new perspective and approach to our old*

OB concepts and some new and exciting core concepts such as confi-
dence, hope, optimism, happiness, and resiliency . . . I have found in
the positive psychology movement what I was looking for to get me
out of my own negativity with the OB field." [3]

Following his transformation, Luthans developed POB, which
stands for "positive organizational behavior." He defines POB as
"the study and application of positively oriented human resource
strengths and psychological capacities that can be measured, developed, and effectively managed for performance improvement
in today's workplace." [4]

A key concept in POB is what Luthans calls psychological
capital (PsyCap), the positive human resources that are of great
value to organizations. [4] PsyCap is open to learning, development
and change, depending on the workplace. Moreover, its effect on
organizational performance is measurable.

Luthans sets a high bar for the inclusion of positive human
resources in PsyCap. Thus far, only four have made the cut. They
are: self-efficacy, hope, optimism and resiliency.

But he believes happiness (or "subjective well-being," as he
calls it) "may best meet the PsyCap inclusion criteria beyond the
four established components of efficacy, hope, optimism and re-
silience." [5] This is because Luthans feels that the "happy worker is
a productive worker" hypothesis is well supported. For example,
an extensive review in the 1990s showed that more-satisfied employees are more cooperative, more helpful to co-workers, more
punctual and efficient and more loyal to the company. [6]

The most compelling evidence to support the "happy worker
is a productive worker" hypothesis comes from a meta-analysis by
the Gallup Organization. Gallup developed a measure of happi-

ness (or "engagement") that includes twelve simple items—such as "My supervisor seems to care about me as a person," "My opinions seem to count," "I have had opportunities to learn and grow." Using this scale and other measures, Gallup surveyed hundreds of workforces around the world. Many organizations provide business-unit-level measures of performance that are comparable from one unit to the next. In total, the database includes about 8,000 business units in 21 different industries with about 200,000 respondents. Results indicate that workplace engagement is positively related to employee productivity, employee retention, customer satisfaction, and, in turn, to profitability and stock value.

Having established that employee happiness is a key element of POB that can help companies deliver positive outcomes, the question arises, "How can we make employees happy?"

THE DRIVERS OF EMPLOYEE HAPPINESS

Consider a 2011 survey conducted by CareerBliss, an online career community and resource dedicated to helping people find joy at work and success in their careers (one of their key online taglines is "find a happier job.") [7] They analyzed hundreds of thousands of employee reviews to determine what makes workers happy. Employees were, of course, concerned about tangible items, but salary was not the number-one concern. Rather, people cared about a comprehensive benefit mix, career advancement and work/life accommodations.

Regarding benefits, one of the companies that scored high in the survey was the cable TV provider Comcast. It offers staff above-average health insurance coverage, dollar-for-dollar 401(k) matching, free financial planning services, life and disability insurance, tuition reimbursement, commuter benefits, legal benefits, adoption benefits, long-term care insurance and pet insurance, as well as free cable TV and Internet and discounted phone service for employees living in a Comcast service area. Sounds like a great total reward package!

Regarding career opportunities, Dr. Jody Heymann, the director of McGill University's Institute for Health and Social Policy and author of *Profit at the Bottom of the Ladder: Creating Value by Investing in Your Workforce,* reports in her book that Costco provides career opportunities for employees at all levels.[8] Committed to growing and developing its employees, the company promotes from within its own workforce 98 percent of the time. This approach rewards employees but also helps the company. Costco's commitment to career opportunities inside the company leads to a very low employee turnover rate compared to that of their competitors.

Finally, work/life accommodations are increasingly important given the increasing number of dual careers. Carlson, a privately held global hospitality and travel company based in Minnesota, has been one of the best companies for working mothers for many years; its flexibility allows for extensive work/life accommodations.[9]

While a great benefit package, career opportunities and work/life balance may be important and beneficial to the employee and the company in the long run, the drivers of employee happiness are more complex, involving a variety of organizational and personal factors. Dr. Peter Warr, emeritus professor at the Institute of Work Psychology at the University of Sheffield and an expert on happiness and unhappiness in work settings, feels that a broad view of environmental and personal features influence happiness.[10] In one of his papers, he lists twelve organizational characteristics that apply to a variety of jobs, from factory worker to manager:[11]

- Opportunity for personal control (discretion, decision latitude, participation and so on).
- Opportunity for skill use and acquisition (the potential for applying and developing expertise and knowledge).
- Externally generated goals, ranging across job demands, underload and overload, task identity, role conflict, required emotional labor and work-home conflict.
- Variety in job content and location, rather than an unchanging input from the environment.
- Environmental clarity (role clarity, task feedback and low future ambiguity).
- Contact with others, in terms of both quantity (amount of contact, irrespective of its personal value) and quality (illustrated negatively and positively as aggression or social support).
- Availability of money (the opportunity to receive income at a certain level).
- Physical security (for example, in factory job settings, this may concern working conditions, degree of hazard and similar themes).
- Valued social position (the significance of a task or role).
- Supportive supervision (the extent to which one's concerns are taken into consideration).
- Career outlook (job security or the opportunity to gain promotion or shift to other roles).
- Equity (justice both within one's organization and in that organization's relations with society).

Moreover, his model takes into account personal factors that determine employee happiness:

- Social comparison with other employees ("How does my situation compare with that of others?").
- Expectations ("How does my situation compare with what I expected?").
- Imagination ("How might the situation have developed in other ways?").
- Time comparisons ("Up till now, has the situation deteriorated, improved or remained unchanged?").
- Role assessment ("Do I want to be in this role?").
- Task attractiveness ("Do I like the things I have to do?").

Finally, in line with the ideas presented in this book, Warr believes that happiness requires multidimensional study. According to him, one dimension runs from feeling bad to feeling good, while two others are distinguished in terms of degree of activation and degree of pleasure. These latter two dimensions range from negative feelings of anxiety to experiences of happiness as tranquil contentment, and from states of depression to happiness as energized pleasure. A given factor may affect only a certain dimension of happiness positively or negatively. For instance, high job demands may affect unhappiness of the anxious kind more than unhappiness of the depressed kind. Also, each dimension may lead to different outcomes—for instance, activated pleasure may lead to more initiative-taking than happiness of a low-arousal kind.

Warr's framework may seem a bit complicated, but I find it quite useful nonetheless. If you would like to explore it further, I encourage you to apply it to your own work situation or those of your colleagues.

However, the framework has a deterministic tone to it, which is incompatible with positive psychology's view of happiness. Rather than looking at an individual's work being influenced by environmental and cognitive forces, and designing these environmental forces accordingly (or getting them to correct their perceptions), one would ideally allow the individual employee more flexibility and choice. This brings up the idea of a customizable career—a concept pioneered at Deloitte, the largest professional services firm in the US.

DELOITTE'S "CUSTOMIZABLE CAREER"

Deloitte is at the forefront of HR (or what they call "talent") management because their very business depends entirely on their people. They see a direct correlation between the firm's ability to grow and the number and quality of their employees.

In the past, climbing the corporate ladder defined career success at a firm like Deloitte. Now there are fewer rungs to grasp and different models of success for organizations and individuals. With this in mind, Deloitte decided to move away from the traditional linear ladder to create a more customized workplace.[12]

The new initiative was spearheaded by Cathleen Benko, vice chairman of Deloitte LLP.[13] Benko is a star in talent and innovation circles, an authority on talent strategies and transformational change to achieve exceptional results. Among many accolades, *Consulting Magazine* named Benko as one of the "25 Most Influential Consultants" and a "Frontline Leader." We first met when she contacted me to talk about how talent management can be used to reinforce the corporate brand, and conversely, how the brand can make employees proud and happy.

"The notion of happiness is a very individual concept. The connection between success and happiness is, I think, a pretty thin line," Benko told me. Deloitte has found that when there's an optimal career/life fit, as perceived by each individual, happiness goes up dramatically. So they have developed a systematic way to scale choices and options that are tailored to the individual, in areas such as how they build their careers, how they do their work and how they participate in the organization. They call the result a "customizable workplace."[14]

Benko believes that a "customizable workplace" is necessitated by major organizational and societal changes.[15] Organizational hierarchies have become 25 percent flatter in recent decades. Workers increasingly have nontraditional family units (and value them), while trying to get ahead in the workplace. The changing roles of working women and the changing views of men toward work are creating additional challenges for employers. There are other employee issues looming in the future, like the increased necessity of elder care and the skilled-labor shortage mentioned earlier.

"Deloitte has moved from being a career destination to being a career enhancer," says Benko. "Some may stay a shorter time, others longer; some may select a partnership track while others will not. Whether an individual chooses to dial up, dial down or stay on a more traditional path, it is okay, as long as there is continual development and expansion of skills, experiences, and relationships." Benko and Deloitte pioneered a "corporate lattice" model to provide a scalable, tailored approach to work.[15] The century-old corporate ladder model was anchored in the goal of scaling efficiency. The ladder represented an inflexible view of advancement, rewards and access to information and power. Everyone wanted the corner office. But in the age of globalization, technology and widespread democratic access to information, the "corporate lattice" offers a more adaptive and flexible way forward, by providing various career pathways.

In other words, employers must not try to hold the new breed of employees too tightly to the one-size-fits-all rules of the past. Rather, they need to empower them to build their careers with a view toward establishing a long-term relationship, even if that employee moves to another company or firm. Employees will no longer be locked into their jobs. As Benko notes, you can "visualize fluidity" within this lattice framework; building a career today is an ever-changing calculus. The corporate lattice offers more ways for the employee to keep contributing by moving upward, sideways, diagonally and even down.

Great companies are not only detail-oriented in considering the myriad factors that matter to employees. They are also authentic when dealing with their employees and create a lively and inspiring workplace for employees in what has been called an "authentizotic organization."[16]

THE "AUTHENTIZOTIC ORGANIZATION"

"Authentizotic" is a neologism. It combines the Greek words *authentikos* (trustful and reliable) and *zotikos* (vital to life), referring to organizations that are authentic and lively.

The term was coined by Dr. Manfred Kets de Vries, a clinical professor of leadership development at the international graduate business school INSEAD and founder of INSEAD's Global

Leadership Center. He's also a psychoanalyst and has authored an original and entertaining book titled *Sex, Money, Happiness, and Death: The Quest for Authenticity,* in which he explores how these existential issues affect our work and our lives.[17] I recommend the book for further reading, but let's stick to his concept of the authentizotic organization for now.

According to Kets de Vries, authentizotic organizations have developed a set of meta-values that allow employees to derive joy and meaning from their work. Such organizations are a source of meaning and growth for employees and are characterized by a spirit of camaraderie, trust, open and frank communication and opportunities for learning and personal development. According to Kets de Vries, authentizotic organizations fulfill three important human needs: a sense of enjoyment, a sense of meaning and a sense of active belonging to a community. Not surprisingly, these three human needs correlate closely with the three types of happiness we outline in this book: pleasure, meaning and engagement.

Kets de Vries's concept of the authentizotic organization adds life and color to some of the historically dry concepts of HR and OB. I fully agree with him that great organizations and high performance teams are characterized by authenticity rather than politics and by vitality rather than a bureaucratic following of procedures.

In my view, authenticity and vitality are most important to the younger generation of employees. They don't like insincerity and politics; they don't draw a firm line between work and leisure. They are redefining the workplace. Their Facebook page is always open while they work; they chat and consult, and have fun, with their friends while at work.

CUSTOMER-FACING EMPLOYEES

So far we have examined HR from the internal perspective of the firm, based on the principle that employee satisfaction contributes to customer satisfaction. This is especially important for customer-facing employees. A customer-happiness-focused firm therefore makes sure that its customer-facing employees feel good and deliver customer happiness. It defines desirable outcomes for customers in its HR policies. The most impressive illustration in this respect has always been the Walt Disney World Resorts. Let's look at people management at their Florida theme park.

WALT DISNEY WORLD RESORT AND ITS CAST MEMBERS

The Walt Disney World Resort has developed its policies and practices with a view toward making sure that the customer experience at the Magic Kingdom is truly magical. And employees are an integral part of the overall strategy to engage and keep customers happy.

"You can dream, create, and build the most wonderful place on earth, but it takes people to make that dream a reality," founder Walt Disney said decades ago.[18]

With more than 45 million visitors each year, the various theme parks comprising Walt Disney World form a small city in central Florida, south of Orlando.[19] Hundreds of miles of roads, 33 resorts and hotels spread across 25,000 acres, about the size of San Francisco, or twice the size of Manhattan Island.

When the Magic Kingdom opened in 1971, there were about 5,500 employees. Now more than 65,000 people work there, taking home over USD 1.2 billion in payroll and USD 474 million in benefits; it's the largest single-site employer in the US.

So the workforce had better be strong, because Disney customers arrive with huge expectations, raised even higher by Disney's powerful advertising and marketing campaigns: people are repeatedly told how great, magical, wonderful and happy it's going to be when they get there.

"You have to deliver because you usually have one, two or three generations coming," said Lee Cockerell, former executive vice president of operations, Walt Disney World Resort, in an interview for this book. "We have the grandparents, parents, and grandkids coming together, so the groups are getting larger."

Employees at the Disney World Resort are called "cast members." They perform a role, not a job. And they are given a clear objective for their role as cast members: create magical moments for the visitors. The remainder of employee training is about the details of how to make it happen.

"We get tens of thousands of letters a year telling us how great we are, but it's never about the attractions or the shows or the rides," says Cockerell. "It's always about how great the employees and cast members are, and how Mary took care of them at 10:00 at night when they had a problem and Mel came back in and got her husband a phone charger from Wal-Mart, and delivered it on his day off. So when you talk about magical, it's not magic that makes Walt Disney World work, it's the way we work . . . we're very careful about who we hire," Cockerell stresses.

Each new cast member, whether a VP or a janitor, spends an entire day learning about Disney traditions and their impact on America, with a view toward understanding that customers want someplace to escape their daily problems and concerns. Over the three-day training period, cast members watch videos, meet with supervisors and do team-building exercises that stress Disney history, corporate values and quality standards. Finally, there is the Walt Disney World International College Program, an internship program that offers American and international college students a chance to live in four Disney-owned apartment complexes and work at the resort. This program produces many of the "front line" cast members.

The customer comments on the Disney blog seem to sum up why they've been so successful in drawing so many customers.[20] It comes down to the role that the cast members plays and their attention to making sure the paying visitors are truly happy.

Steve, May 30th, 2011

"I was at Disney & on this trip took my mother. We were staying at the animal kingdom lodge & she left her wedding rings in the room after we had checked out. She cried and was so upset, as they couldn't be replaced. Robert @ the animal kingdom lodge found our room information & address and mailed them to her & to this day she tells the story. :)"

Samantha, May 30th, 2011

"We went to Disney for the very first time in April. Every cast member was spectacular, but the one that stood out the most did this: We were in Hollywood studios waiting for the Jedi training academy. While we were waiting, we purchased frozen popsicles for our family. My son had eaten a small amount when the Popsicle broke and fell on the floor. He of course started to cry and I went to give him mine. Out of nowhere, one of the cast members came over to comfort him and said 'Don't worry, I'll get you a new one' She gave him a new Popsicle. It made him so happy."

Patricia, May 30th, 2011

"When we were eating at the Port Orleans Riverside Food Court, a cast member chose our son, along with some other kids, to be Junior Chefs. My son got to wear the chef's attire and decorated a cookie with a variety of toppings. This was a magical moment for him (as he was only 2 years old at the time) and for us as well. I love the magic of Disney!"

Cast members routinely give this type of extra attention to heighten the customer experience. It shows that Disney employees are highly motivated and trained to ensure that guests leave the parks with a big smile.

Working at Disney may be fun, especially when you can put a smile on a child's face. But can the customer-focused approach be replicated at other workplaces that are less fun? Take call centers, often considered one of the worst work environments. Can they be transformed into happy places?

THE TELEPERFORMANCE CALL CENTER IN BRAZIL

Call centers have a bad image. They are arguably one of the most demanding, stressful and unhappy work environments. The job itself is often part-time, and employees are generally paid only minimum wage. Most of the calls handled by the agents are about problems. Conversations with customers can easily get emotional and tense; it is not uncommon for customers to scream at agents. The physical environment is often sterile and depressing, and there is pressure to answer as many calls as possible in a day.

As a result, employees are often deeply dissatisfied, and absenteeism and attrition rates are abysmal. It is difficult to deliver customer satisfaction with disgruntled employees. And because they don't see the return on their investment, companies push call-center providers to further cut costs because they view call centers as a necessary evil rather than a value-add. The call-center company, in turn, pushes its employees even harder. There seems to be no way out of this vicious cycle.

Teleperformance is a worldwide leader in outsourced call and contact centers. In 2010, it had more than 130,000 employees and reported revenues of USD 2.8 billion. Recently, it tried to break the mold by offering a premium call-center product: Teleperformance Platinum. The one in Brazil has become a stunning success. In fact, Teleperformance in Brazil was voted one of the top five employers in that country across a wide range of industries.

Paulo César Vasques was in charge of setting up the new call center in Brazil. I met him at a speaking engagement for the company. They hired me for my expertise in experience marketing and management because they wanted to create a desirable employee experience.

What did Vasques do to create the "platinum experience"? "What I did was not rocket science. I just focused on treating call-center employees with respect, being close to them, provided opportunities for them and created a comfortable environment for them. For us they are the first customers of the company, they're the ones who provide the greatest impact," he told me.

In other words, he went back to the basics. First, offer the call-center employees a career, not just a short-term job. Second, pay them an above-average salary. Third, give them the right job (that is, match their interests to the client they are serving). Vasques also changed the performance metric to "first call resolution." Thus, the agent is empowered to spend time with a caller until a problem is solved, rather than trying to get off the phone to answer another call. Moreover, when things get emotional, an audio measurement can detect it in the caller's and agent's voices and automatically notify a supervisor to take over.

Finally, Vasques completely changed the work environment. The Platinum Experience Center in Brazil is not a sterile, hospital-like room with white walls. It's comfortable, almost elegant. The walls are colorful and decorated. There are windows and spaces to relax and have fun. There are entertainment programs at the facility. In other words, the environment is very different from most other call centers.

I asked Paolo Righetti of GN Research, the research arm of Teleperformance, about the results. "We have more competent staff, less absenteeism and more loyal staff. The clients are much happier as well because the end-user experience is better. The relationship between employee satisfaction and client satisfaction is a solid correlation of 0.78," he noted.

THE PHYSICAL ENVIRONMENT

The physical work environment at a call center can play a key role in employee happiness. For call-center employees, the physical environment is critical because their jobs are fairly routine and they occasionally need a nice break.

Many other companies today also understand the importance of the physical environment. Google, with its "Googleplex" concept, has become the benchmark for creative environments. Bloomberg's New York offices, with their clear walls, are a good benchmark for "high tech" environments and comfortable break areas. I have seen environments that integrate tradition and innovation in creative ways (Munich Re, the reinsurance company, for example) as well as environments that integrate their product and brand lines creatively in the office (several consumer packaged goods companies). Everywhere, I see more pool, Ping-Pong or foosball tables. Creating environments to help stimulate happy feelings among employees seems to be a trend.

The environment is equally important for staff that travels a lot, such as middle and senior managers. In their case, the physical work environment can extend far beyond one office. In Germany, there's an environment that has been set up to provide a happy, productive environment for just this target group of traveling executives.

NEW WORK CITY

The Squaire is a live-work-play zone set up in the middle of Frankfurt Airport City, adjacent to the actual airport. It promotes itself as a "New Work City."

Some 660 meters long, 65 meters wide and 9 stories high, it is a blend of office space, conference facilities, a business club, high-quality restaurants, hotels and shopping, as well as recreation and relaxation opportunities—all sitting atop Frankfurt Airport's long-distance train station. The Squaire is part of Frankfurt Airport City, a public and privately funded collection of offices and amenities, including the Gateway Gardens, a former US military base that was given back to Germany in 2005. [21]

Never mind the awkward spelling of "Squaire" or the tacky allusion to "New York City" (Germans just love New York City!), this EUR 1 billion project is part of an effort to position Frankfurt as the new center of gravity for European travel and commerce while providing a great experience for those who work there.

The location, with direct access to Europe's second biggest airport, InterCity Express trains and the autobahn, is very convenient. The architecture is fresh and exciting. More importantly, it's a complex designed for companies and their people who are looking for a working environment that suits their needs. Offices are state-of-the-art; many are designed as satellite offices for the employee that steps in and out. Dry cleaners and hair stylists are a short walk from the office. Because offices are located next to a vast forest, people have a green environment to look at and a place to jog. Art displays and live entertainment are offered in the light-suffused atria.

"New Work City" is aimed at international clientele who work and play in Frankfurt today, London tomorrow and Shanghai the day after that. Executives flying through can maximize their time between flights with a client meeting, a meal with business partners, some shopping or a workout. The idea is to help improve the work-style of the business traveler and give them more opportunities to be happy both during and outside of work. [22]

In sum, the Squaire is designed to draw international companies into setting up regional or international headquarters around the airport. Transport and mobility are its strengths, and the city hopes to go head-to-head with international metropolises in Europe, the Middle East and Far East—places like Amsterdam, Dubai and Hong Kong. Completed in fall 2011, occupancy rates already exceed 80 percent.

CONCLUSION

There is solid evidence that happy employees are productive employees. Moreover, happy employees are more likely to make their customers happy. That's why it is in the best interest of companies to understand what makes employees happy and to create environments that will allow them to experience happiness. As we've seen, there are many factors that affect employee happiness—from tangible benefits to social-environmental factors to the physical space.

In the last chapter of this book, we will be on the lookout for happy citizens. That is, we turn from customer and employee happiness to the topic of citizen happiness. How can governments help their citizens live full and rewarding lives?

9

HAPPY CITIZENS ANYWHERE?

Happiness is no longer just a customer or employee issue. Governments and national leaders are now jumping on the happiness bandwagon. They are increasingly concerned about making their citizens happy—and not merely to increase per capita income. Happiness, as a concept and desired outcome, has reached the level of government planning.

So, where are the happy citizens—or, more revealingly, where are citizens the happiest? To answer this question, we need a reliable and valid measure of happiness that can be administered globally. So far, such a measure does not exist. However, since the turn of the century, when the positive psychology movement put happiness on the agenda, there have been several developments toward creating such measurements and drawing a world map of happiness. Let's take a look at some of these approaches.

A WORLD MAP OF HAPPINESS

In 2006, a study by Adrian White, an analytic social psychologist at the University of Leicester in England, drew media attention.

White analyzed data published by UNESCO, the CIA, the New Economics Foundation, WHO (World Health Organization), the Veenhoven Database, the Latinbarometer, the Afrobarometer and the UNHDR (United Nations Human Development Report), to create a global estimation of subjective well-being.[1] His meta-analysis was based on the findings of over 100 different studies that included 80,000 people around the world.

The 20 happiest nations were: Denmark, Switzerland, Austria, Iceland, the Bahamas, Finland, Sweden, Bhutan, Brunei, Canada, Ireland, Luxembourg, Costa Rica, Malta, the Netherlands, Antigua and Barbuda, Malaysia, New Zealand, Norway and the Seychelles. The three least happy places were all in Africa: the Democratic Republic of the Congo, Zimbabwe and Burundi.

Note that most of the 20 happiest countries are relatively small in terms of population. Many of the larger countries do not perform as well. The US ranked 23rd, China 82nd, India 125th and Russia 167th.

What mattered, and correlated strongly with the level of happiness of each nation, was health levels (correlation of .62), GDP per capita (.52), and provision of education (.51). These three measures in and of themselves are strongly interrelated; together, they may be considered the basics of citizen happiness.

Alex Davies, a doctoral student at Cambridge University, used quite a different approach to assess the happiness of nations. He created the Twitter Happiness Map, assessing moods around the world based on tweets.[2] His map is based on a text-mining methodology (a "semi-supervised hierarchical mixture-of-multinomials model"). Germany came out number 1, followed by the Netherlands, Mexico, the US and Denmark. The map also displays happiness for US states. Tennessee came out on top while New York ranked 14th.

There are other indices. For example, the Happy Planet Index (HPI) measures the ecological efficiency with which well-being and happiness are delivered worldwide.[3] To put it simply, the index weighs life expectancy and life satisfaction against carbon footprint. On this measure, Costa Rica, the Dominican Republic and Jamaica are leading. The 2009 report notes that we are far away from achieving "sustainable happiness," that is, delivering long and happy lives without overstretching the planet's resources.

Finally, the New Economics Foundation (NEF), an independent "think-and-do tank" of economists, has called for national measures and accounts of well-being. They have measured personal and social well-being across European nations, using many of the concepts of positive psychology such as positive feelings, self-esteem, vitality, supportive relationships and trust (among others). Overall, Denmark, Switzerland and Norway came out on top in both summary measures of personal and social well-being.

None of these approaches are perfect; all have methodological problems. Samples are often not representative or comparable across nations. Also, social norms may differ with respect to expressing moods and emotions in general, especially in surveys or tweets. These factors could distort the results.

We are only at the beginning of appropriately measuring the happiness of citizens in different countries. Depending on the measure, countries rank in quite different positions.

Despite these measurement issues, citizen happiness has become part of the government agenda in France, Canada and the UK. All three are determined to launch projects that make their citizens happier. The basics of citizen happiness—income, healthcare and education—clearly play a role. Indeed, incomes and GDP, in particular, were considered the Holy Grail for decades. But, interestingly, income only seems to matter up to a certain level; after that, the relationship between income and happiness is at best spurious—a phenomenon we called the Easterlin Paradox in chapter 1. It was named after Professor Richard Easterlin of the University of Southern California, who first discovered the phenomenon.

THE EASTERLIN PARADOX AND ITS CAUSES

In a classic article in the 1970s, Easterlin observed that economic growth may not improve the human lot as much as previously thought.[4] Whereas, in a given country, people with higher incomes report being happier, the reported level of happiness across nations does not vary much with national income per person when a certain basic level is achieved. Most importantly, although income per person rose strongly in the US after World War II, happiness did not. In fact, it declined in the 1960s. The government policy implications of these findings is that policy should not focus on economic growth alone once certain basic needs are met.

The Easterlin Paradox does have its critics. Some authors have published data showing a steady rise in happiness, albeit much more slowly above a certain point. In 2010, Easterlin presented new data from a sample of 37 countries that seem to reaffirm the paradox. He also defended his position and explained why other researchers may have found different results.

"There are several reasons but the principal one is that they mistake a short term positive association between well-being and GDP per capita for the long-term relationship. In major economic contractions and expansions, life satisfaction tends to follow the V-shaped pattern of GDP per capita, resulting in a positive association between the two over the short term. This is demonstrated most dramatically by the countries that have been undergoing economic transitions since around 1990. But when the time span of the analysis is lengthened to the point where these short term movements cancel out, the positive relation between happiness and GDP per capita disappears. There is, therefore, good reason to regard the Easterlin paradox as alive and well as a problem for classical economic theory."[5]

The finding that money does not make you happier, or at least not much happier, beyond a certain point is puzzling to economists. After all, it should. Money can be exchanged for almost anything and can thus be spent on things that make you happy.

But not only economists believe that income and happiness should be closely linked; ordinary people believe this, too. Why is that? Dr. Daniel Kahneman, a psychologist who was awarded the Nobel Prize in Economics in 2002, and his co-authors have addressed this question.[6] They examined a range of activities and asked people how happy each of these activities made them, using their own "day reconstruction method" (remembering daily episodes and indicating how happy you were at these moments).

At the top of the scale were social activities such as intimate relations (aka sex), socializing and relaxing. Somewhere in the middle of the scale was shopping; work and commuting were at the bottom. People are happiest, it turns out, with friends, relatives and spouses. They are less happy with co-workers or their bosses. They then argued that when people think about higher incomes, they may think about the additional possessions they could afford and the leisurely pursuits they could enjoy. But they may neglect to think about what it takes to make more money: working, spending more time with the boss, and sacrificing time spent socializing. In other words, people's beliefs about the relationship between income and happiness are subject to what they called a "focusing illusion."[7]

If more money does not make you (much) happier after a certain income level, is there anything else that does? And if there is, could governments provide it on a broad scale and make citizens happier? The studies by Kahneman suggest that social activities might help. But there may be other factors as well. Let's look at a government-initiated project that I encountered in Singapore.

MARINA BAY: SINGAPORE'S "GARDEN CITY BY THE BAY"

I'm checking into an apartment at "The Sail @ Marina Bay" an hour after having my iced latte near the intersection of Orchard and Scotts Roads. The Sail is Singapore's tallest residential building (245 meters). Many executives who travel in and out of Singapore live here. I am not only amazed by the view but also how simple and easy everything is in this building—and in Singapore.

Within five minutes, Starhub, the local information and communication provider, has me online. Five minutes later I am set up for a TV plan; in another couple of minutes my mobile is working, and the Japanese air conditioners hum away, cooling the sultry Singapore day. When my visitors press the call button to visit me, there is no outdated intercom; I buzz them into the building by pressing "1#" on my mobile. The public transportation system underground runs to the minute. Singapore citizens can get through airport immigration in 30 seconds by using their fingerprints. Seems like a modern, happy life.

I decided to live in the Sail because I wanted to be in an area where I could truly experience the best of what the new Singapore has to offer. It's easy for me to walk to the metro, shops, restaurants and cultural activities at the nearby Esplanade Theatres by the Bay. The concert hall is top-notch; part of the wooden structures can be tilted to customize the sound for each orchestra and then stored away for their next visit. The acoustics are superb (I have tested it with Mahler's First and Seventh Symphonies). I also enjoy walking near the water where a mist sculpture installation piece and huge motion-activated fans refresh passersby.

The Sail is part of a development project called Marina Bay, Singapore's wholly manufactured, utterly planned "Garden City by the Bay." In less than a decade, the 890-acre (360-hectare-) area has morphed from a rather desolate open patch of grass and water that people drove past on their way to someplace else to a vibrant focal point for a city on the rise.[8] Now sparkling new office towers and luxury apartments look down on the generous waterfront promenade, al fresco dining spots, and an "integrated-resort" casino complex with convention center, museum, restaurants, shopping and a "Skypark." The change is nothing short of breathtaking, especially considering that the entire area sits on reclaimed land.

Nothing here is left to chance. Everything from the type, size and placement of buildings, utilities, green space and roads to the type, size and color of trees and shrubs (unique planting schemes differentiate the individual districts) has been meticulously thought out to make Marina Bay a "beacon for change and progress" according to Singapore's Urban Redevelopment Authority (URA), the agency largely responsible for its master plan. Even the colors on the official logo represent different elements of the area: a place to explore (orange), exchange (magenta) and entertain (green). The blue logo center represents the bay as a focal point for the area. There's also underground infrastructure like rail transportation, shopping and pedestrian walkways linking Marina Bay to the central business district. A "Common Services Tunnel" houses electrical, telecommunication cables and other utilities that make future road digging unnecessary. They've thought of everything. [9]

The government talks about Marina Bay being designed with a specific identity that does not focus on land or the buildings, but rather on people and "how they explore, exchange and entertain." The area is discussed as a global brand for "24/7 live, work and play," the way any savvy marketer or ad man would discuss a consumer product that they're trying to sell. [10] With government investment in the project at around SGD 5 billion (approximately USD 4 billion), it's easy to believe that the primary reason behind developing this area is economic and not just people-centric.

When I met the CEO of the URA, Ng Lang, at a social event (the Formula One night race), he gave me his business card with the inspiring brand slogan underneath the logo, "To make Singapore a great city to live, work and play in."

As the infrastructure hardware for the area is being developed, the URA also set up the Marina Bay Development Agency to focus on the software for developing the area. [11] It has pushed ahead with a full marketing and promotions campaign and developed activities to draw people and publicity. Tens of billions of foreign investment dollars are flowing in. The calendar of events for public spaces, nearby roads, and the water is already generating buzz. Signature events have included a New Year's Eve Countdown, the annual National Parade, the annual Formula One night race, dragon boat races, kite-flying days, music concerts, the Standard Chartered Singapore Marathon and any number of half marathons, 10K races and fun runs. Plus, there is a nightly laser show at the integrated resort.

Interestingly, the other major partner in this project is the Singapore Tourism Board. They clearly recognize that this area should and will be a key driver in attracting tourists, conventioneers and business people, encouraging them all to leave their money behind. Already the Marina Bay Sands Casino, shops and restaurants are drawing record crowds and mind-blowing quarterly profits, making it a bigger cash cow than the Sands property in Las Vegas.

But can this manufactured fun and experience zone lead to happiness for citizens of the city-state? Will watching the fireworks, the laser show or flying a kite do the trick? Is this what governments can contribute to happiness?

Let's look at some of the psychological thinking that has emerged over the last ten years to address these questions. As we will see, psychologists are keen to address the "big picture" issues of happiness and discuss the implications of their findings on public policy. Consumer-behavior researchers, too, are moving toward addressing citizens, and not just consumer happiness. Let's consider some of the most relevant research that has been conducted in this area.

EXPERIENCE VS. POSSESSIONS

Professors Leaf Van Boven and Thomas Gilovich, both psychologists, wrote an article with an intriguing title, "To Do or To Have? That Is the Question"—meaning is the good life better lived by doing things or by having things? [12] They answer the question by comparing "experiential purchases" with "material purchases."

Tom Gilovich was one of my advisors in the doctoral program in psychology at Cornell University. His main interest is the study of judgment and decision making. I am delighted to see that he has branched out into the expert area of his former pupil (me): consumer behavior and experiential marketing.

Van Boven and Gilovich define "experiential purchases" as those made with the primary intention of acquiring a life experience: an event or a series of events one lives through (such as travel, going to a concert or skiing). In contrast, "material purchases" are defined as purchases with which consumers acquire a material good, a tangible object that is kept in their possession (such as a watch, clothing or computer equipment).

They then conducted a national phone survey of 1,279 Americans, aged 21 to 69, asking them to think of an experiential and a material purchase with the aim of increasing happiness, and to indicate which of the two purchases made them happier. The result: experiences made people significantly happier than possessions (57 percent versus 34 percent—the remaining percentages indicated that they were not sure). Importantly, they found this effect across a variety of demographic categories (age, type of employment, ethnicity, gender, marital status, political affiliation, region and residential environment). It does not matter much if you are young or old, a student or employed, white, African American or Asian, male or female, single or married, a Democrat or a Republican or even where you live. The overwhelming effect is that experiences make us happier than "stuff."

Why is this? Van Boven and Gilovich suggested that experiences may be more central to one's identity, more memorable and more pleasurable to talk about. Experiences foster social relationships. "Communities will have happier citizens if they provide for facilities that create experiences, such as ski resorts, hiking trails or arts centers," Gilovich told me.

I like the conclusion: experiences matter to people; they are fundamental for our happiness; governments should take experiences seriously. Marina Bay in Singapore provides a lot of experiences for its residents and visitors. In fact, having experiences rather than acquiring possessions is what the area is mostly about. Naturally, there is luxury shopping in the casino complex, but aside from that it is primarily an event area, a garden on the bay, a live, work and play environment.

More generally, I am all for ski slopes, hiking trails and—as an opera buff and art collector—supporting the arts. But I am also mindful that not every citizen shares my eccentric taste for obscure operas of the German repertoire with lots of (artistic) nudity. There are citizens who prefer to have their memorable experiences at sports events (olé! olé! olé!), and they often don't get their tastes supported by public money. In fact, spectator sports seem to be the one thing that's missing from Marina Bay . . . but I hear that will change.

In fact, when a country is awarded a major sporting event, say, the Soccer World Cup, it can be a valuable tipping point for urban development. That's what Qatar, the nation that will host the 2022 Soccer World Cup, will do. Qatar, a small country and not exactly a soccer nation, has come up with a brilliant idea to make sure that its citizens can enjoy the experience and that the stadiums won't be empty after the tournament. The stadiums will be built in a modular way so that they can easily be dissembled and shipped to nations in need of new stadiums (Nigeria, for example). The idea: create happy experiences for your citizens, improve your image in the world and perhaps even get a foothold in resource-rich emerging markets.

My only concern with the Van Boven and Gilovich argument is the well-defined dichotomy between experiences and possessions, and its humanistic and anticommercial undertones. In my own work on experiential marketing, I have argued that anything can be experiential. A watch can be experiential if you savor its aesthetics. Clothing, especially fashion items, certainly are. Even computers can be experiential (see Apple). So it may not be the nature of the thing itself (experience versus possessions) but rather *how* experiential the possessions or experiences are.

To prove this point, I recently conducted a study, with Lia Zarantonello and J. J. Brakus, two frequent collaborators of mine, on the relationship between the degree of experience, happiness and quality of life.[13] We conducted a diary field experiment, using Kahneman's "day reconstruction method" described earlier.

Participants filled out their diaries in the evening to report their daily consumption experiences ("eating or preparing food," "entertaining yourself," "engaging in physical activities," "grooming and dressing" and "shopping"). As we expected, the degree of experience was indeed significantly correlated with happiness and with perceived quality of life.

In sum, experiences as well as experiential possessions can make people happy. The Marina Bay project discussed earlier is just one way in which governments can create citizen happiness. But Marina Bay was created from scratch. What about existing infrastructure? Can you transform it to have the desired impact? Let's look at an experience project in Los Angeles.

L.A. LIVE

Downtown Los Angeles. The mere mention of the place, for most people, conjures up images of gangs, drugs, homeless people and violence. Indeed, following a short golden age in the 1920s, after World War II, downtown L.A., like many other downtown areas in the US, gradually declined as residents bought cars and moved to the suburbs. Investment in the once-wealthy area decreased. Low-income or no-income housing became the norm. Between 1930 and 1960, numerous buildings were demolished and replaced by street-level parking lots. For many Angelinos, downtown became a place where you went during working hours to do your business, then got out.

Like many other people, I had quite a negative image of downtown L.A. and avoided the area on my frequent trips to the city. Recently, when a client put me up in the JW Marriott in downtown for a speaking engagement, I thought "Oh, my God!" But I was surprised to witness an incredible urban revival that has taken place in the area over the last few years. There is Frank Gehry's fabulous Walt Disney Concert Hall, the Staples Center, home of the Los Angeles Lakers basketball team, and, coming soon, the Wilshire Grand Tower, a supertall skyscraper expected to break ground in 2012.

I was most impressed with the immediate area where I was staying. The JW Marriott belongs to L.A. Live, a 5 million-square-foot entertainment and lifestyle entertainment complex next to the Staples Center. L.A. Live, which opened in 2007, cost approximately USD 2.5 billion and was mainly developed by Anschutz Entertainment Group, one of the largest sports and entertainment groups, with some help from the city and its taxpayers.

On a 27-acre (10.9-hectare) site, the complex includes apartments, restaurants, bars, movie theaters and a 54-story hotel and condominium tower. It has two world-class hotels, the JW Marriott and the Ritz-Carlton, and a central plaza next to the Staples Center. The so-called Nokia Plaza serves as a broadcast venue with large LED screens and a red carpet site for special events. There are also the Nokia Theatre, a music and theater venue seating 7,100 people, the Grammy Museum and the ESPN Zone and broadcasting studios.

L.A. Live, like Marina Bay in Singapore, is a lifestyle and experience concept. The website is organized around three themes: "Eat," "Play" and "Stay" as well as an event calendar listing sports and music events.[14] You find the usual suspects here: a Starbucks (actually a very nice one!) and an Espressamente Illy for the Europhiles; Wolfgang Puck, the L.A.–based global Austrian American celebrity chef is present with two restaurants—Wolfgang Puck Bar and Grill, serving contemporary American cuisine, and WP24 Restaurant & Lounge, on the 24th floor of the Ritz-Carlton Hotel, offering stunning panoramic views of downtown and beyond. L.A. Live is truly transformational and experiential for downtown Los Angeles.

There are also other notable smaller-scale developments in the area. In the past decade or so, warehouses have been turned into chic lofts, and there is more and more pedestrian-friendly retail. Former residents are coming back, including higher-income individuals and families.

There are plans to connect the Staples Center and L.A. Live to the Disney Concert Hall, City Hall, and the future Wilshire Grand to create an even larger, concentrated and walkable urban center. Finally, there is a plan for a 72,000-seat, USD 1.2 billion NFL stadium and dozens of ultrabright LED billboards. These new projects are being criticized by neighborhood groups and local activists who don't want the area to lose too much of its character. I guess they don't want it to turn into a "perfect-planned" Singapore.

EXPERIENTIAL THIRD PLACES

Aside from Marina Bay in Singapore and L.A. Live, there are numerous experiential projects, many in Asia: Malaysia's Putra Jaya government complex in Kuala Lumpur and the Iskander development in Johor, Shanghai's Pudong, the Kotai Strip in Macao, or Tokyo's Shiodome, Roppongi Hills and Tokyo Midtown. All of them were created over the last 15 years. In Europe, I recently consulted for a Belgian real-estate project developer, Uplace, which creates such projects all over Europe. Here is how they describe what they do on their website:

> *"Uplace 'third places' are experience destinations where people continuously discover new sources of inspiration. They provide today's time-strapped consumers the opportunity to interact, to play, to shop, to live, to love and to learn, all in one place . . . Uplace looks*

beyond bricks and buildings. Reflecting our goal of urban revital-
ization, Uplace sets out to provide a real answer to individual,
community and city needs. Our work places meet the unique de-
mands of companies and their employees. Our experience desti-
nations combine everything a city and its inhabitants have been
missing in one go-to spot. In short, Uplace is about building places
where people love to be." [15]

The concept of "third place" used by Uplace is associated with Professor Ray Oldenburg, an urban-sociology professor from Florida.[16] Oldenburg calls the home one's "first place" and work one's "second place." "Third places" are informal places that anchor community life and create community vitality. They serve important societal needs and provide citizens with a sense of belonging. The hallmarks of a third place are that it is free or inexpensive, that food and drinks are available, that it is easily accessible, that it is welcoming and that it is a place to spend time with friends. The concept has been applied to pubs, social clubs, bowling alleys, beauty parlors, community centers and coffeehouses (in fact, Starbucks calls itself a third place).

Experiential lifestyle places like Marina Bay in Singapore, L.A. Live and the ones created by Uplace in Europe combine various third places under one roof, so to speak, thus creating a "mega-third place." They are innovative, and not just in terms of scale. They provide variety and allow for multiple activities and events. In the planning and construction stages, they involve multiple constituencies and bring together diverse communities. Their nature also attracts lifestyle brands, such as Starbucks, Wolfgang Puck, Adidas, and the like, which offer experiential retailing and turn the acquisition of possessions into fun. At these experiential places, one not only eats and drinks, but also shops and hangs out. This can certainly contribute to a good and happy life.

So, around the world, public and private organizations are looking to set up experiential lifestyle places to create better and happier lives for citizens. Besides providing opportunities for experiences, what else can governments do to make their citizens happy? One answer: help them focus on time rather than money.

THINK TIME, NOT MONEY

Besides money, the other major resource that people (and consumers) have in their lives is time. Time in many ways is like money: an important, scarce resource you can either save or lose. But time is also different in important ways. Time gains may not be as valuable as money gains, and time losses cannot be as easily made up for. In general, time is less fungible and substitutable than money; it cannot easily be transferred or recouped. This may make it an even more precious resource than money, especially when an individual has few options for how to allocate his or her free time.[17]

Free time, unlike money, has not increased for Americans. Americans are working harder and harder. Europeans, in contrast, have decreased the number of work hours and generally seem to be less concerned about how to make and spend money than how to spend their leisure time. Interestingly, happiness levels in Europe have increased.[18] So, increases in free time and happiness seem correlated, but is the relationship a causal one? Are Europeans happier because they work less?

Professor Cassie Mogilner of the University of Pennsylvania's Wharton School explored the relationship between time, money and happiness. Mogilner conducted two behavioral experiments that examined causation.[19] In one study, with more than 300 adults, she asked people to complete a questionnaire with various activities and asked them how happy these activities would make them. As usual, people said that the activities that would make them most happy were connecting activities (socializing and sex); those that would make them less happy were independent activities (working and commuting). She also asked the participants to focus on either time or money. When they focused on time, people were more motivated to engage in activities that they said would make them happy. However, when they focused on money, they were more likely to engage in activities that they said would make them less happy.

Interestingly, she replicated this effect with a separate sample of a low-income population and found the same effect. Thus, even those who have less money might be happier if they focused on time rather than money. Of course, as Mogilner suggests, because they have to worry about how to make ends meet, they often have no time to do so.

In another study, Mogilner did not merely ask what people wanted to do but observed what they actually did, for example, in a café. At a place like Starbucks you can socialize and relax, or you can work. When customers entered the café, Mogilner had them focus on time or money, then observed what they did in the café. As they left half an hour later, she asked them how happy they felt. Those who focused on time spent more time socializing (talking to others, talking on the phone) and less time working (for example, on a laptop). And the reverse was true for those who focused on money: they spent less time socializing and more time working. Most importantly, Mogilner showed that, owing to the activities in which they had engaged, customers who focused on time were happier when they left the café than those who had focused on money.

Interestingly, some participants in the study were not asked to focus on either time or money. In this neutral condition, participants reported the same happiness levels as those in the money condition. Thinking about money may be the default for Americans, the preferred thinking style, and this may prevent them from being truly happy.

Mogilner concludes:

> *"It seems that money may be more frequently primed in America than in Europe, and that interpersonal relationships and happiness suffer as a consequence. Perhaps our culture and society should shift the focus away from money, and in turn be happier."*

HAPPINESS AS CHOICE

In addition to experiences versus possessions, and thinking about time rather than money, there are other individual, societal and cultural factors that may affect happiness. And some of the above recommendations may not work for everyone. There are people who don't enjoy socializing. There are people who love work. There are people who, when they suddenly have a lot of time (e.g., because they retire), don't know what to do with it. There are cultures that value money greatly, but in a playful way.

Ultimately, citizen happiness is about choice—having the choice of where to live, having the choice of which job to take, having the choice to work long hours and perhaps into old age, having the choice to express your views and having choices as consumers.

In my classes, I ask my students—typically adults in their twenties—to talk about three products or brands that make them truly happy. You may want to ask yourself the same question: Which brands delight you, create joy in your life? Which ones are you attached to? Which brands make you truly happy—and why? I am always amazed at the variety of product categories and brands that my students mention.

They talk about Apple, of course, and some of the products and brands that I covered in this book: Coca-Cola, Red Bull, W Hotels, Brita. But they also mention many others and why these brands make them happy: TripAdvisor (because of the useful reviews), Netflix (because of the level of customization in suggesting relevant movies), Zappos (because of the great service and the surprising little freebee like a Red Bull drink with the delivery), Nike (because they allow me to design my own shoes), Odwalla juice (because of their integrity: no preservatives, no sugar added, all natural), Sephora (because the store experience completely engages me), Zipcar (because it makes renting a car fun) and the Pinkberry frozen yogurt chain (just wonderful!). They also talk about new media brands such as the location-based social networking site Foursquare (because of connecting with friends), the online storage brand Dropbox (because it allows me to collaborate easily with my classmates), Google (because it is a first stop for efficient research of any kind)—and many more. As you can see, their "why" responses echo many of the core concepts in this book.

More than that, these responses indicate that having choices as consumers seems to be part of living a happy life.

CONCLUSION

Citizen happiness depends on certain societal basics: a certain income, health and level of education. Beyond that, money, in particular, does not seem to guarantee happiness.

Rather, living a life full of experiences and focusing on how to spend one's time in a pleasurable, meaningful and engaging way seem to be critical for long-term happiness.

To guarantee a basic level of happiness, governments must contribute to securing societal basics. Beyond that, they can enhance the happiness of their citizens by engaging them at third places where people may experience joyful and meaningful events and activities, as ordinary individuals and as consumers.

Most important, citizen happiness and customer happiness are deeply intertwined. Having choices among a variety of consumer goods and services, and being able to choose whether or not to shop till you drop, is part of living a happy life. Consumers seem to be most happy when they can derive pleasure and meaning from these choices and when companies truly engage them.

NOTES

CHAPTER 1

1. "Happy Meal," Wikipedia, http://en.wikipedia.org/wiki/Happy_Meal.
2. Ben Paynter, "Making Over McDonald's," Fast Company, October 1, 2010, http://www.fastcompany.com/magazine/149/super-style-me.html.
3. "Happy Banking—an Initiative from Bankwest," Bank of Western Australia, http://www.bankwest.com.au/about-us/welcome-to-bankwest/welcome-to-bankwest/happy-banking.
4. "Having a Happy Period," Always, Procter & Gamble Company, http://www.always.com/period/haveahappyperiod.jsp.
5. Beinggirl.com, http://www.beinggirl.com/?legacyurl=/en_US/pages/home.jsp.
6. "Always and Forever," Snopes.com, http://www.snopes.com/humor/letters/always.asp.
7. "Forget GDP: Happiness Is the Secret of Success," Guardian (UK), September 20, 2009, http://www.guardian.co.uk/business/2009/sep/20/economics-wealth-gdp-happiness.
8. "Happiness Economics," Wikipedia, http://en.wikipedia.org/wiki/Happiness_economics.
9. Ed Diener, "Subjective Well-being: The Science of Happiness and a Proposal for a National Index," American Psychologist, 2000.
10. "Net Promoter Score," Absolute Astronomy, http://www.absoluteastronomy.com/topics/Net_promoter_score.
11. Richard Oliver, Roland Rust, and Sajeev Varki, "Customer Delight: Foundations, Findings, and Managerial Insight," Journal of Retailing 73, issue 3, pp. 311-336, 1997.
12. Frederick F. Reichheld, "The One Number You Need to Grow," Harvard Business Review, December 1, 2003. http://www.hbr.org.
13. "Rethinking the Social Responsibility of Business: A Reason Debate Featuring Milton Friedman, Whole Foods' John Mackey, and Cypress Semiconductors' T. J. Rodgers," Reason.com, October 2005, http://reason.com/archives/2005/10/01/rethinking-the-social-responsi.

CHAPTER 2

1. The Happy Company, http://www.thehappycompany.com/.
2. Happy Mountain Farm, http://www.minicattle.com/entry.cfm.
3. The Happy Cooperative, http://www.thehappycooperative.org/.
4. Darrin M. McMahon, *Happiness: A History* (New York: Atlantic Monthly Press, 2006).
5. Darrin M. McMahon, "A History of Happiness: We've Forgotten Much of What Older Traditions Knew about Happiness," *Yes!*, October 2, 2010, http://www.yesmagazine.org/happiness/a-history-of-happiness.
6. Arthur Schopenhauer, *The World as Will and Representation,* trans. and ed. Judith Norman, Alistair Welchman, and Christopher Janaway (Cambridge and New York: Cambridge University Press, 2010).
7. Darrin M. McMahon, "The Pursuit of Happiness in Perspective," *Cato Unbound,* April 8, 2011, http://www.cato-unbound.org/2007/04/08/darrin-m-mcmahon/the-pursuit-of-happiness-in-perspective/. Darrin M. McMahon, "The History of Happiness," *Arts & Opinion* 10, no. 1. 2011, http://artsandopinion.com/2011_v10_n1/mcmahon-happiness.htm.
8. Ed Diener, Robert A. Emmons, Randy J. Larsen, and Sharon Griffin, "The Satisfaction with Life Scale, " *Journal of Personality Assessment* 49, no. 1 (1985), http://www.unt.edu/rss/SWLS.pdf.
9. Marilyn Elias, "Psychologists Now Know What Makes People Happy," New York Times, September 10, 2009, http://www.biopsychiatry.com/happiness/.
10. McMahon, "A History of Happiness."
11. Christopher K. Hsee, Yang Yang, Naihe Li, and Luxi Shen, "Wealth, Warmth and Well-being: Whether Happiness Is Relative or Absolute Depends on Whether It Is About Money, Acquisition, or Consumption," *Journal of Marketing Research* 46, no. 3 (June 2009), http://www.marketingpower.com/AboutAMA/Pages/AMA%20Publications/AMA%20Journals/Journal%20of%20Marketing%20Research/TOCs/SUM_2009.3/Wealth_Warmth_Well-Being.aspx.
12. C. K. Prahalad, *The Fortune at the Bottom of the Pyramid: Eradicating Poverty through Profits,* 5th ed. (Upper Saddle River, N.J.: Wharton School Publishing, 2010).
13. Abraham Maslow, *Motivation and Personality* (New York: Harper and Row, 1954).
14. Fred Luthans, "The Need for and Meaning of Positive Organizational Behavior," *Journal of Organizational Behavior* 23 (2002): 695-706.
15. "FAQ on the Science of Happiness," The Pursuit of Happiness, http://www.pursuit-of-happiness.org/science-of-happiness/faq-on-science-of-happiness/.
16. Martin E. P. Seligman, *Flourish: A Visionary New Understanding of Happiness and Well-being* (New York: Free Press, 2011).
17. Victor E. Frankl, *Man's Search for Meaning,* rev. ed. (New York: Washington Square Press,1984).
18. Mihaly Csikszentmihalyi, *Flow: The Psychology of Optimal Experience* (New York: Harper and Row, 1990).
19. "Chocolate Invented 3,100 Years Ago by the Aztecs—but They Were Trying to Make Beer," Mail Online, November 13, 2007, http://www.dailymail

.co.uk/news/article-493335/Chocolate-invented-3-100-years-ago-Aztecs
—trying-make-beer.html.

20. "Cocoa Year 2010/11," *ICCO Quarterly Bulletin of Cocoa Statistics* 37, no. 2 (2011).

21. Kristen Morris and Douglas Taren, "Eating Your Way to Happiness: Chocolate, Brain Metabolism, and Mood," *Karger Gazette,* no. 68, http://www .karger.com/gazette/68/morristaren/art_3.htm.

22. "The Chocolate Industry," International Cocoa Organization, http://www .icco.org/about/chocolate.aspx.

23. Sacred Chocolate, http://www.sacredchocolate.com/home.php.

24. Knipschildt Chocolatier, http://www.knipschildt.net/la-madeline-au-truffe .html.

25. Morris and Taren, "Eating Your Way to Happiness."

26. "2008 Toyota Prius," HybridCar.com, October 21, 2007, http://www.hybrid car.com/index.php?option=com_content&task=view&id=521&Itemid=103.

27. "Half Gas, Half Electric, Total California Cool: Hollywood Gets a Charge Out of Hybrid Cars," Washington Post, June 6, 2002, http://www.washingtonpost .com/ac2/wp-dyn?pagename=article&node=&contentId=A2587-2002Jun5.

28. "Celebrity Hybrid Drivers," HybridCar.com, March 24, 2006, http://www .hybridcars.com/hybrid-drivers/celebrities.html.

29. "Oil Warrior: Former CIA Chief James Woolsey Says If You Want to Beat Bin Laden, Buy a Prius," *Motor Trend,* May 2007, http://www.motortrend .com/features/112_0705_james_woolsey_interview/index.html.

30. Skype Numerology, http://skypenumerology.blogspot.com/2011/03/number -of-skype-users.html.

31. "Skype," Wikipedia, http://en.wikipedia.org/wiki/Skype.

32. Melanie Lasoff Levs, "Video Conferencing: More New Options," Mother Nature Network, http://www.mnn.com/green-tech/research-innovations /stories/video-conferencing-more-new-options.

33. Laura Furr, "Facebook, Skype Merger to Compete with New Google+," lsurev- eille, http://www.lsureveille.com/entertainment/facebook-skype-merger-to -compete-with-new-google-1.2606802.

34. Samuel D. Gosling, Peter J. Rentfrow, and William B. Swann Jr., "A Very Brief Measure of the Big-Five Personality Domains," *Journal of Research in Personality* 37 (2003): 504-528, http://homepage.psy.utexas.edu/HomePage /Faculty/Gosling/tipi%20site/JRP%2003%20tipi.pdf.

35. David E. Gard, Marja Germans Gard, Ann M. Kring, and Oliver P. John, "Anticipatory and Consummatory Components of Experience of Pleasure: A Scale Development Study," *Journal of Research in Personality* 40 (2006): 1086-1102, http://socrates.berkeley.edu/~akring/Gard%20et%20al%202006.pdf.

36. Robert R. McCrae, "Aesthetic Chills as a Universal Marker of Openness to Experience," Springer Science+Business Media, 2007, http://ahealthymind .org/csg/Members/Aesthetic%20chills%20openness%20McCrae07.pdf.

37. Prudential, http://www.prudential.com.sg/corp/prudential_en_sg/prestige/in dex.html.

38. Justin L. Epstein, The Center on Global Brand Leadership, interview with Ken Kim, Director of Brand Communications for ILI at Prudential Financial, August 10, 2011.

39. Giselle Tsirulnik, "Godiva Launches Mobile Application for Chocolate Sales," Mobile Marketer, May 5, 2008, http://www.mobilemarketer.com/cms/news /commerce/936.html.
40. "In Action: Godiva Chocolate Email Marketing," 708 Media: Website Design and Marketing, August 8, 2010, http://www.708media.com/online _marketing/in-action-godiva-chocolate-email-marketing/.
41. "Godiva Mobile!: Order from Godiva Anytime, Anywhere!," Godiva Chocolatier, http://www.godiva.com/promotions/godiva_mobile.aspx.

CHAPTER 3

1. "About W," W Hotels Worldwide, http://www.starwoodhotels.com/whotels /about/index.html.
2. Ibid.
3. "Experience," W Hotels Worldwide, http://www.starwoodhotels.com/w hotels/experience/whatwhen.html.
4. Alexander Berzon, "Hilton Paid Starwood $75 Million in Espionage Settlement," Wall Street Journal Online, http://online.wsj.com/article/SB1000142 4052748703652104576121721433277798.html.
5. Meryl Gordon, "The Cool War: Ian Shrager vs. His Imitators," *New York Times,* May 27, 2001, "Ian Schrager," Cityfile New York, http://cityfile.com /profiles/ian-schrager.
6. "Inside the Newly Opened Aloft Harlem," Hotel Chatter, http://www.hotel chatter.com/story/2011/2/4/151636/3915/hotels/Inside_the_Newly _Opened_Aloft_Harlem.
7. Morten L. Kringelbach, "The Functional Neuroanatomy of Pleasure and Happiness," Discovery Medicine, June 25, 2010, http://www.discovery medicine.com/Morten-L-Kringelbach/2010/06/25/the-functional -neuroanatomy-of-pleasure-and-happiness/.
8. Fred B. Bryant and Joseph Veroff, Savoring: A New Model of Positive Experience (New York: Lawrence Erlbaum Associates, 2006).
9. Illycaffè, http://www.illy.com.
10. Le Pain Quotidien, http://www.lepainquotidien.com/.

CHAPTER 4

1. "Yoga," Wikipedia, http://en.wikipedia.org/wiki/Yoga.
2. "About Yoga Works," http://www.yogaworks.com/about.aspx.
3. Earth Power Yoga, http://www.earthspoweryoga.com/.
4. "Top 25 Yoga Studios Around the World," *Travel + Leisure,* http://www .travelandleisure.com/articles/25-top-yoga-studios-around-the-world/1.
5. Air Yoga, http://www.airyoga.ch/zuerich.html.
6. TriYoga, http://www.triyoga.co.uk/.
7. "About Us," The Yoga Institute: Santacruz, Mumbai, http://www.theyoga institute.org/about_us.htm.
8. Sivananda Yoga Vedanta Centre, http://www.sivananda.org/delhi/home.php.
9. Victor E. Frankl, *Man's Search for Meaning: An Introduction to Logotherapy* (New York: Washington Square Press, 1963).

10. S. H. Schwartz, "Are There Universal Aspects in the Content and Structure of Values?," *Journal of Social Issues* 50, no. 40 (1994): 19–45.

11. Sonia Roccas, Lilach Sagiv, Shalom H. Schwartz, and Ariel Knafo, "The Big Five Personality Factors and Personal Values," *Personality and Social Psychology Bulletin* 8, no. 6 (June 2002), http://www.scribd.com/doc/28366479/The -Big-Five-Personality-Factors-and-Personal-Values.

12. This case was originally published in 2009 by Columbia CaseWorks of Columbia University (www4.gsb.columbia.edu/caseworks) as case number 090519 and is used with permission.

13. "How to Go Green: Water," Tree Hugger: A Discovery Company, http: //www.treehugger.com/files/2006/12/how-to-go-green-water.php.

14. Peter H. Gleick and Heather S. Cooley, "Energy Implication of Bottled Water," Pacific Institute, http://www.pacinst.org/reports/bottled_water/index.htm.

15. "IBWA Rebuts Misleading and Faculty Incorrect Video about Bottled Water," International Bottled Water Association, http://www.bottledwater.org/news /ibwa-rebuts-misleading-and-factually-incorrect-video-about-bottled-water.

16. "Brita," Wikipedia, http://en.wikipedia.org/wiki/Brita.

17. BRITA, http://www.brita.com/a-better-you/.

18. BRITA, "Learn the Facts," http://www.filterforgood.com/facts/.

19. Ibid.; "Brita," Wikipedia; Tree Hugger, "Brita Water Filter Ad Campaign Provokes Strong Reactions," http://www.treehugger.com/files/2008/05/brita -water-filter-ads.php.

20. Schwartz, "Are There Universal Aspects in the Content and Structure of Values?"; Sheena Iyengar, *The Art of Choosing* (New York: Hachette, 2010).

21. "Our Vision," Philips, http://www.philips.com.sg/.

22. Uniqlo, http://www.uniqlo.sg/product.html#/UT.

23. "BlackBerry Smartphones Sales Decline Makes It 'Broken Brand' Says *[sic]* Trade Analysts," Cool Avenues.com, March 28, 2011, http://www.cool avenues.com/companies/tech-news/blackberry-smartphones-sales-decline -makes-it-broken-brand-says-trade-analysts.

24. "Bottled Water: Pure Drink or Pure Hype?," Natural Resources Defense Council, http://www.nrdc.org/water/drinking/bw/exesum.asp.

25. Tree Hugger, "How to Go Green: Water," http://www.treehugger.com/htgg /how-to-go-green-water.html.

26. "What Is a Smarter Planet?" IBM, http://www.ibm.com/smarterplanet/us /en/overview/ideas/index.html?re=CS1.

27. Walter Robb and Margaret Wittenberg, "USDA Disappoints: No Regulations on GE Alfalfa," *Whole Story: The Official Whole Foods Market Blog* (blog), January 28, 2011, http://blog.wholefoodsmarket.com/2011/01/no -regulations-ge-alfalfa/.

CHAPTER 5

1. "Coca-Cola Happiness Machine US," YouTube, http://www.youtube.com /watch?v=lqT_dPApj9U; "Coca-Cola Happiness Machine London," You Tube, http://www.youtube.com/watch?v=M0D3jKLz6sA&NR=1.

2. "The Coca-Cola Friendship Machine," YouTube, http://www.youtube.com /watch?v=Bj3QLLTFDX8.

3. "Coca-Cola Happiness Truck," YouTube, http://www.youtube.com/watch ?v=hVap-ZxSDeE.
4. "Coca-Cola Happiness Store," YouTube, http://www.youtube.com/watch?v =CMgxJguVw2Y&feature=relmfu.
5. Joe Fernandez, "Coca-Cola Launches Latest 'Open Happiness' Campaign Online First," *Marketing Week,* February 4, 2011, http://www.marketing week.co.uk/sectors/food-and-drink/soft-drinks/coca-cola-launches-latest -open-happiness-campaign-online-first/3023123.article.
6. Stuart Elliott, "Tropicana Discovers Some Buyers Are Passionate about Packaging," New York Times, February 22, 2009, http://www.nytimes.com /2009/02/23/business/media/23adcol.html?_r=1&ref=business.
7. Jessica Mousseau, "Why Are Videos Games So Popular Today?," Associated Content, January 11, 2007, http://www.associatedcontent.com/article /114606/why_are_video_games_so_popular_today.html.
8. Jeremy Porter, "A Look at How People Share Content on the Web," Journalistics, July 30, 2009, http://blog.journalistics.com/2009/how-people-share -content-on-the-web/.
9. "The New York Times Completes Research on 'Psychology of Sharing,'" The New York Times Company, July 13, 2011,http://phx.corporate-ir.net /phoenix.zhtml?c=105317&p=irol-newsArticle&ID=1584873.
10. Simon Warburton, "Global Lingerie Market Sees Uplifting Forecast," Just-Style, January 12, 2010, http://www.just-style.com/analysis/global-lingerie -market-sees-uplifting-forecast_id106393.aspx.
11. Ibid.
12. "Gendered Fashion, Power, and Sexuality: A History of Lingerie," Random History, http://www.randomhistory.com/1-50/028lingerie.html.
13. Marsha West, "Victoria's (Dirty Little) Secret," Renew America, November 30, 2007, http://www.renewamerica.com/columns/mwest/071130.
14. "Victoria's Secret Pink," eBay, http://reviews.ebay.com/Victoria-apos-s -Secret-Pink_W0QQugidZ10000000007662050.
15. Monica Khemsurov, "Sexing Up Victoria's Secret: The Lingerie Retailer's Revamped New York Flagship Signals a New Look for Malls Nationwide, Bringing Once-Stuffy Store Design into Step with the Brand's Supermodel Image," CNN Money, April 1, 2004, http://money.cnn.com/magazines /business2/business2_archive/2004/04/01/366224/index.htm.
16. "M and S Lingerie Ads Banned from Outdoor Promotion Due to 'Provocative' Content," AndhraNews.com, May 17, 2011, http://www.andhranews .net/Intl/2011/M-S-lingerie-ads-banned-outdoor-8309.htm#ixzz1UWhr CpHX.

CHAPTER 6

1. Bernd Schmitt and Alex Simson, *Marketing Aesthetics* (New York: Free Press, 1997).
2. "OpentheDoorofIntimacyandEnteraNewWorldofRomance,"Amazon(UK), http://www.amazon.co.uk/gp/feature.html?ie=UTF8&docId=1000215213.
3. Dual Sensual Massagers, Philips, http://www.philips.co.uk/c/sensual -massagers/for-him-and-her-hf8400_00/prd/.

4. Kerry Capell, "Philips Unveils Massager for Couples, BusinessWeek, September 8, 2008.

5. "Duet," CKIE, http://www.ckie.com/project/duet.

6. "National Geographic Store at Vivo City in Singapore," Design Boom, http://www.designboom.com/weblog/cat/8/view/5848/national-geographic-store-at-vivo-city-in-singapore.html.

7. "Welcome to the National Geographic Store," http://www.worldwideretailstore.com/.

8. Tony Hsieh, *Delivering Happiness: A Path to Profits, Passion and Purpose* (New York: Hachette, 2010).

9. Virgin Galactic, "News," http://www.virgingalactic.com/news/item/nasa-selects-virgin-galactic-for-suborbital-flights/.

10. "Virgin Galactic," Wikipedia, http://en.wikipedia.org/wiki/Virgin_Galactic.

11. Saul McLeod, "Social Identity Theory," Psychology Academic Articles for Students, 2008, http://www.simplypsychology.org/social-identity-theory.html.

12. "Dove Campaign for Real Beauty," Wikipedia, http://en.wikipedia.org/wiki/Dove_Campaign_for_Real_Beauty.

13. Bernd Schmitt, *Big Think Strategy: How to Leverage Bold Ideas and Leave Small Thinking Behind* (Cambridge, Mass.: Harvard Business School Press, 2007).

14. Michelle Miller, "Hot Gossip: Dove to Dump 'Real Beauty' Campaign," Wonder Branding, March 30, 2011, http://www.wonderbranding.com/2011/03/hot-gossip-dove-to-dump-real-beauty-campaign/.

15. "Citi-Mobile Launches Mobile Billboard Campaign for the New Perfect One Bra by Victoria's Secret," www.prweb.com/releases/2009/prweb2214114.htm.

16. This case was originally published in 2009 and updated in 2011 by Columbia CaseWorks of Columbia University (www4.gsb.columbia.edu/caseworks) as case number 090503, and is used with permission.

17. "Wikipedia," Wikipedia, http://en.wikipedia.org/wiki/Wikipedia.

18. "Mobile Payment," Wikipedia, http://en.wikipedia.org/wiki/Mobile_payment.

19. Lia Zarantonello and Bernd Schmitt, "The Impact of Events on Brand Equity," working paper, Columbia Business School, 2011.

20. "Red Bull Gives You Social Media Wings," Ice Cream (Media), http://icecreamsocialmedia.wordpress.com/2010/10/28/red-bull-gives-you-social-media-wings/.

21. David L. Rogers, *The Network Is Your Customer: 5 Strategies to Thrive in a Digital Age* (New Haven, Conn.: Yale University Press, 2011).

22. Chorus, http://www.getchorus.com/.

23. Ibid.

24. Ibid.

CHAPTER 7

1. C. K. Prahalad, *The Fortune at the Bottom of the Pyramid: Eradicating Poverty through Profits*, 5th ed.(Upper Saddle River, N.J.: Wharton School Publishing, 2010).

2. Jennifer Reingold, "Can P&G Make Money in Places Where People Earn $2 a Day?," *CNN Money*, January 6, 2011, http://features.blogs

.fortune.cnn.com/2011/01/06/can-pg-make-money-in-places-where-people -earn-2-a-day/.

3. "Can't We Design a Better Hospital Room?," Glimmer Site, August 22, 2009, http://glimmersite.com/2009/08/22/cant-we-design-a-better-hospital -room/reboot/.

4. "The Consumer's Voice—Can Your Company Hear It?," The Boston Consulting Group (BCG), November 2009, http://www.bcg.com/documents /file35167.pdf.

5. This case was originally published in 2010 by Columbia CaseWorks of Columbia University (www4.gsb.columbia.edu/caseworks) as case number 100505 and is used with permission.

6. Samsung, http://www.samsung.com/us/.

7. Sea-Jin Chang, *Sony vs. Samsung: The Inside Story of the Electronics Giants' Battle for Global Supremacy* (Singapore and Hoboken, N.J.: Wiley, 2008.)

CHAPTER 8

1. David McCann, "To the 'Three R's' Add One More: Writhing; Companies Will Feel Ever More Pain as the Shortage of Technically Skilled Workers Intensifies," *CFO Magazine*, March 1, 2011, http://cfo.com/article .cfm/14557286/1/c_14557613?f=search.

2. Stephen R. Covey, *The Seven Habits of Highly Effective People: Restoring the Character Ethic* (New York: Simon and Schuster, 1989).

3. Fred Luthans, "The Need for and Meaning of Positive Organizational Behavior," *Journal of Organizational Behavior* 23 (2002): 695-706.

4. F. Luthans, "Positive Organizational Behavior: Developing and Managing Psychological Strengths," *Academy of Management Executive* 16, no. 1 (2002): 57-72, page 59.

5. Paul E. Spector, *Job Satisfaction: Application, Assessment, Cause, and Consequences* (Thousand Oaks, Calif.: Sage Publications, 1997).

6. "Factors Impacting Employee Happiness," Northwestern Benefits Corporation of Georgia, August 22, 2011, http://www.northwesternbenefit.com /News/IndustryNews/tabid/88/articleType/ArticleView/articleId/79 /Factors-Impacting-Employee-Happiness.aspx.

7. Career Bliss, http://www.careerbliss.com/.

8. Jody Heymann with Magda Barerra, *Profit at the Bottom of the Ladder: Creating Value by Investing in Your Workforce* (Boston: Harvard Business Press, 2010).

9. "Carlson Recognized as One of the 100 Best Companies for Working Mothers," Carlson News Releases, September 15, 2011, http://www.carlsonhotels .com/news-and-media/news-releases.do?article=4465397.

10. Peter Warr, *Work, Happiness, and Unhappiness* (Mahway, N.J.: Lawrence Erlbaum, 2007).

11. Rev. Psicol., Organ, Trab. v.7 n.2 Florianópolis dez. 2007.

12. "The Corporate Lattice: An Interview with Cathleen Benko, Vice Chairman and Chief Talent Officer, Deloitte LLP," Leaders Online, http://www .leadersmag.com/issues/2011.3_Jul/ROB/LEADERS-Cathleen-Benko -Deloitte.html.

13. "Cathy Benko," Deloitte, http://www.deloitte.com/view/en_US/us/Insights /Browse-by-Content-Type/people_profiles/sorter/cathy_benko/index.htm.

14. Ibid.

15. Cathleen Benko and Molly Anderson, The Corporate Lattice: Achieving High Performance in the Changing World of Work (Boston: Harvard Business Review Press, 2010.)

16. Manfred Kets de Vries, "Creating Authentizotic Organizations: Well-Functioning Individuals in Vibrant Companies," Human Relations 54, no. 1 (2001): 101-111.

17. Manfred Kets de Vries, *Sex, Money, Happiness, and Death: The Quest for Authenticity* (Basingstoke and New York: Palgrave Macmillan, 2009).

18. "Walt Disney Quotes," Just Disney, http://www.justdisney.com/walt_disney /quotes/.

19. "Walt Disney World Fun Facts," http://corporate.disney.go.com/media /news/Fact_WDW_Fun_Facts_08_06.pdf.

20. Disney Park Blog, http://disneyparks.disney.go.com/blog/2011/05/disney -cast-members-create-magic-every-day/.

21. Gateway Gardens, http://www.gateway-gardens.de/en/areal.html.

22. "Frankfurt Airport Becomes Airport City: The Squaire, Europe's Largest Commercial Property, Is Under Construction, " December 15, 2010, http://www .frankfurt.de/sixcms/detail.php?id=8657&_ffmpar%5b_id_inhalt%5d=7597 117.

CHAPTER 9

1. "Denmark 'Happiest Place on Earth,'" BBC News, July 28, 2006, http://news .bbc.co.uk/2/hi/5224306.stm.

2. Alex Davies, "Twitter Happiness Map," http://alexdavies.net/?page_id=558.

3. "Happy Planet Index," NEF, http://www.neweconomics.org/projects /happy-planet-index.

4. Richard A. Easterlin, "Does Economic Growth Improve the Human Lot?" in *Nations and Households in Economic Growth: Essays in Honor of Moses Abramovitz*, ed. Paul A. David and Melvin W. Reder (New York: Academic Press, 1974).

5. "National Accounts of Well-being," NEF, http://www.nationalaccountsof wellbeing.org/.

6. Daniel Kahneman, Alan B. Krueger, David A. Schkade, Norbert Schwarz, and Arthur A. Stone, "A Survey Method for Characterizing Daily Life Experience: The Day Reconstruction Method," *Science* 306 (2004): 1776-1780.

7. Daniel Kahneman, Alan B. Krueger, David A. Schkade, Norbert Schwarz, and Arthur A. Stone, "Would You Be Happier If You Were Richer? A Focusing Illusion," *Science* 312 (2006): 1908-1910.

8. "Creating a 'City-in-a-Garden,'" Urban Redevelopment Authority, News Releases, March 6, 2006, http://www.ura.gov.sg/pr/text/pr06-10.html.

9. Ching Tuan Lee and Benjamin Ng, "Realising the Marina Bay Vision," *Business Times*, March 22-23, 2008, http://www.marina-bay.sg/BT _22-23Mar08%28pg7%29_Realising%20the%20Marina%20Bay%20vision .pdf.

10. "Marina Bay—A Milestone in Singapore's Future," Urban Redevelopment Authority, News Releases, July 21, 2005, http://www.ura.gov.sg/pr/text/pr05 -29.html; "Marina Bay—Garden City by the Bay," Marina Bay Singapore, Vision, http://www.marina-bay.sg/vision.html.

11. Ching Tuan Lee and Benjamin Ng, "Realising the Marina Bay Vision."

12. Leaf Van Boven and Thomas Gilovich, "To Do or To Have? That Is the Question," *Journal of Personality and Social Psychology* 85, no. 6 (2003): 1193-1202.

13. Lia Zarantonello, J. J. Brakus, and Bernd Schmitt, "Experience, Happiness and Quality of Life," Working Paper, 2011.

14. L.A. Live, http://lalive.com/.

15. "About UPlace," UPlace, http://www.uplace.eu/default.aspx?PageID=15.

16. Ray Oldenburg, *The Great Good Place: Cafés, Coffee Shops, Community Centers, Beauty Parlors, General Stores, Bars, Hangouts, and How They Get You through the Day* (New York: Paragon House, 1989).

17. France Leclerc, Bernd Schmitt, and Laurette Dube, "Waiting Time and Decision Making: Is Time Like Money?," *Journal of Consumer Research* 22 (1995):110-119.

18. Richard Layard, *Happiness: Lessons from a New Science* (New York: Penguin, 2005).

19. Discussion of Mogilner's work from author interview. See also Cassie Mogilner, "The Pursuit of Happiness: Time, Money, and Social Connection," http://knowledge.wharton.upenn.edu/papers/download/011911_Mogilner 2010TimeMoneyandSocialConnection.pdf.

GENERAL INDEX

COMPANY AND BRAND INDEX

50, 67, 84-85, 96, 111
128, 133, 136

BIG THINK STRATEGY